D0909399

Massacre at Cheyenne Hole

Cadet Austin Henely is seated here for his class-album portrait at West Point in 1872. This is the only known photograph of the officer who, three years later, led the attack on a band of Southern Cheyennes that came to be known as the Sappa Creek Massacre. Courtesy, Kansas State Historical Society.

Massacre at Cheyenne Hole

Lieutenant Austin Henely and the Sappa Creek Controversy

John H. Monnett

The University Press of Colorado

1999

Copyright © 1999 by the University Press of Colorado
International Standard Book Number 0-87081-527-X

Published by the University Press of Colorado
P.O. Box 849
Niwot, Colorado 80544

The University Press of Colorado is a cooperative publishing enterprise supported, in part, by Adams State College, Colorado State University, Fort Lewis College, Mesa State College, Metropolitan State College of Denver, University of Colorado, University of Northern Colorado, University of Southern Colorado, and Western State College of Colorado.

The paper used in this publication meets the minimum requirements of the American National Standard for Information Sciences—Permanence of Paper for Printed Library Materials. ANSI Z39.48-1984

Library of Congress Cataloging-in-Publication Data

Monnett, John H.
    Massacre at Cheyenne Hole : Lieutenant Austin Henely and the Sappa
Creek controversy / by John H. Monnett.
        p. cm.
    Includes bibliographical references and index.
    ISBN 0-87081-527-X (hc. : alk. paper)
    1. Henely, Austin. 2. Sappa Creek (Kan. and Neb.), Battle of,
1875. 3. Cheyenne Indians—Wars. 4. Cheyenne Indians—Government
relations. 5. Massacres—Kansas—Rawlins County—History—19th
century. 6. Henely, Austin. 7. United States. Army. Cavalry,
6th—History. I. Title.
E83.875.M66   1999
973.8'2—dc21   99-10853
                                                              CIP

08 07 06 05 04 03 02 01 00 99   10 9 8 7 6 5 4 3 2 1

For Dad

Contents

Introduction

On the morning of April 23, 1875, H Company, 6th U.S. Cavalry attacked and destroyed a temporary Indian camp located on the Middle Fork of Sappa Creek, a tributary of the Republican River in what is today Rawlins County, Kansas, southeast of the modern town of Atwood.* The ensuing engagement was the last important military action fought on the central plains between an element of the regular U.S. Army and an independent band of Indians composed principally of Southern Cheyennes.†

Commanding H Company in the field during the fight at Sappa Creek was Second Lieutenant Austin Henely, West Point class of 1872. At twenty-six, the handsome, articulate Irish immigrant had served as an officer of the 6th Cavalry on the Kansas frontier since 1872.[1] During that period,

---

* On old section maps, the battleground is located on the southwest corner of the northwest quarter and the northwest corner of the southwest quarter, Section 14, township 5 south, range 33 west, in Clinton Township, Rawlins County, about thirty rods east of the west line of the section. The camp and battlefield covered about forty acres. The remains of the ghost town of Achilles, Kansas, is very near the actual site of the fighting. See *Transactions of the Kansas State Historical Society* 10, no. 4 (1907–1908): 369.

† A few Southern Cheyennes fought with the Northern Cheyennes and Lakota during the Great Sioux War of 1876–1877. A brief skirmish occurred on October 27, 1875, south of the Smoky Hill River between a detachment of the 5th Cavalry and a party of Cheyennes. These Indians were returning from the north to the reservation in Indian Territory. They did so successfully. A number of engagements were fought in Kansas in 1878, including the Battle of Punished Woman's Fork, but these fights were between the army and the Northern Cheyenne bands led by Little Wolf and Dull Knife.

Lieutenant Henely, a bachelor, sent a portion of each paycheck to his financially strapped mother in Chicago.[2]

Henely's victory over the Southern Cheyenne camp of about sixty people—mostly members of the Suhtai band under a warrior named Little Bull, and possibly some members of the Aorta band under a Southern Council chief, Sand Hill (including women and children)—ended the significant fighting in the Red River War with the last holdouts of the reservation Cheyennes of Indian Territory (Oklahoma). The Indians Henely attacked on Sappa Creek had recently fled Indian Territory after a skirmish broke out at the Darlington Agency. A blacksmith under the direction of Lieutenant Colonel (Brevet Major General) Thomas "Beau" Neill, 6th Cavalry, had attempted to place leg irons on alleged ringleaders of the Red River conflict in order to send them to prison at Fort Marion, Florida. When Little Bull and his band, which had not surrendered, discovered the panic following this engagement, known as the Sand Hill fight, they bolted from Indian Territory. When Henely caught up with them, the escaping Cheyennes were camping on the Middle Fork of Sappa Creek.* They were on a leg of a frantic journey to find refuge among the Lakota and their Northern Cheyenne brethren near Red Cloud Agency in Nebraska and eventually, the Powder River country.

Guided to the Indian camp by several Kansas buffalo hunters and Homer Wheeler, a post trader and rancher at Fort Wallace, all of whom joined the troopers in the attack, Henely's subsequent victory was complete and decisive. Henely reported that his command killed twenty-seven Indians—nineteen warriors and eight women and children, "unavoidably killed by shots intended for the warriors."[3] Two troopers of H Company were killed, and none were wounded.[4] The Indian casualties were the highest sustained in any engagement of the Red River War.[5] Following the rout of Little Bull's people, Henely's men plundered and burned the Cheyenne camp, including the corpses of the Indians killed in the fight.

---

* There is much confusion over which fork of the Sappa the Indians were camped on. Henely states in his report that it was the North Fork, whereas others claim it was the middle fork. Actually, the North Fork is extremely short and of little consequence in comparison to the creek's other forks. Henely may not have been aware of the existence of the small North Fork, which even today does not appear on official highway maps.

Returning to Fort Wallace in the teeth of a spring snowstorm, Henely quickly drafted his official report of the engagement, a concise, articulate summary that vividly demonstrated the meticulous sense of detail and duty instilled in an officer educated at the United States Military Academy. Nowhere in his report did Henely use the then commonly accepted term "savage" in recounting the actions of the Cheyennes. Upon recommendation of the Fort Wallace post commander, Major H. A. Hambright, 19th Infantry, the engagement at Sappa Creek won Henely praise from Brigadier General John Pope, commander of the Department of the Missouri, and General of the Army William T. Sherman. Upon Henely's recommendation, the United States eventually awarded eight Medals of Honor to enlisted men of H Company who participated in the battle.

However, years after the event, intimations began to surface that atrocities had been committed at Sappa Creek. In 1908 William D. Street, an early resident of Oberlin, Kansas, who visited the battle site shortly after the fight, published an article in *Transactions of the Kansas State Historical Society* stating that the event was a "terrible tragedy enacted that April morning out on the Kansas plains, where women and babies met their deaths through the vicissitudes of war."[6] Street asserted that one of Henely's troopers later told the story that "what was supposed to be a roll of plunder was carelessly tossed into a roaring fire of tepees and tepee poles, when an outcry told them that the roll contained a living human being, a little Indian papoose."[7] In the same article, the historical society's editors hinted, based on a letter (dated August 17, 1905) sent to the society by Hill P. Wilson, the sutler at Fort Hays, Kansas, in 1875, that details of the plundering of the Cheyenne camp might have been suppressed. It was "understood," Hill wrote, "that the least said about the affair the better for all concerned."[8]

In 1909 another Kansas settler, named F. M. Lockard, who apparently knew some of the buffalo hunters who had participated in the fight on Sappa Creek, published an article further advancing the argument that atrocities were committed. Lockard claimed that several times the Indians tried to parley, sending out flags of truce with some of their women, and each time the Cheyenne women were shot down. After the fight, Lockard asserted, surviving Cheyennes hiding from the soldiers in their lodges "were dragged out, clubbed into insensibility and thrown into the fire. One of the scouts [buffalo hunters] told me," Lockard wrote, "that it was the most cruel and heart rending scene he had ever witnessed, that when the smell of burning flesh reached him, he turned aside and went to camp."[9]

Street's and Lockard's claims are in total contradiction to assessments of Henely's conduct recalled in reminiscences published in 1925 by a participant in the fight, Homer Wheeler, and in the memoir of Sergeant Marcus M. Robbins of H Company, who was a private at the time, and one of the engagement's eight Medal of Honor winners.[*]

Surely the most widely read popular account of the fight at Sappa Creek was published in 1953. Heavily influenced by Street and Lockard, Mari Sandoz in *Cheyenne Autumn* portrayed the alleged atrocities committed as almost unparalleled since the Sand Creek Massacre.[10]

Sandoz also places a number of important Southern Cheyennes at Sappa Creek who could not have been present, particularly Medicine Arrows (Stone Forehead), the keeper of *Maahotse*, the sacred medicine arrows. Sandoz sets the death of Medicine Arrows at Sappa Creek in her book. In later years, Cheyenne historian Father Peter John Powell, using Indian testimony obtained by George Bent and ethnohistorians George Bird Grinnell and George Hyde, has cast serious doubt on Sandoz's claim of Medicine Arrows's death, and on her version of the Sappa Creek story.[11]

The atrocity-massacre version of the fight at Sappa Creek did, however, gain some support in 1958 with the publication by an obscure local press (the local newspaper) in Williams, Arizona, of the reminiscences of Sergeant Frederick Platten, 6th Cavalry. Platten was one of the Medal of Honor winners in the Sappa Creek fight. Platten's account is the only original source that points a finger directly at Austin Henely and suggests that he may have been involved in atrocities. Platten accuses his commander of ordering him to shoot down a defenseless Cheyenne woman and her baby after the fight.[12]

By the 1960s, with the wave of revisionism that began changing the way western history was written, particularly the much needed interpreta-

---

[*] Homer Wheeler's *Buffalo Days* is a highly regarded account of Wheeler's life on the military frontier, including his crucial role in the Sappa Creek fight. Marcus M. Robbins's reminiscences were published in an early volume recounting the actions of the U.S. Medal of Honor winners titled *Deeds of Valor*.

tions of the Indian wars from the indigenous point of view, the accepted thesis concerning the fight at Sappa Creek became that the conflict was a Sand Creek Massacre in microcosm. That viewpoint also predominated in the popular press. Several writers based articles on the Street-Lockard connection. One of the most flagrant examples appeared in 1963, an unsubstantiated article about the fight published in *Real West* magazine, by Gene Jones. Jones described Lieutenant Henely's behavior as psychotic.[13] To lesser degrees, as will be examined in later chapters, this basic perception still persists in some popular accounts in the 1990s.

The only scholarly article to aim at objectivity was published in 1968. G. Derek West, in a piece titled "The Battle of Sappa Creek, 1875," reconstructs the fight and its causes. Much of the article, however, is a critical essay discussing West's assessment of the source material on Sappa Creek. West categorizes the sources as being either "pro-Henely" or "anti-Henely."[14] West is quite clear in his belief that the evidence presented by the anti-Henely sources is "based on gossip and hearsay, combined with deep-rooted prejudice and emotionalism . . ."[15] West also contended that "little of consequence has become available from, or been preserved by the Indians. Dr. Mari Sandoz," West asserted,

> found that discussion of the fight . . . was still largely taboo. Either this taboo still prevails, or the details have become blurred with the passage of time, for when the present writer [West] made an inquiry on the matter, no information was forthcoming. In the first instance, therefore, one must accept the accounts given by white participants of this engagement, which resulted in a minor but overwhelming victory for the United States Army.[16]

Consequently, West's synthesis and evaluations are largely one-sided and somewhat judgmental only toward anti-Henely "evidence." Although West correctly pointed out major errors and inconsistencies in these sources, he failed to examine in depth the major theme that was consistent among most of these admittedly prejudiced sources: that Cheyenne noncombatants, particularly a small child, may have been overtly murdered when H Company, 6th Cavalry, acting on Lieutenant Henely's orders, burned the camp, and that Cheyennes who had come out under a flag of truce to parley with the whites were shot down by the troopers and the buffalo hunters. These consistencies, although neither disproved by West nor proven by his predecessors, carry enough weight to warrant further critical examination. The Sappa Creek controversy has wider meaning never considered in the search for specific crimes. Specifically, why, despite reliable evidence to the contrary, do the atrocity and massacre stories still persist? Are they valid, after all? Were previous researchers ignorant of new material that came to light more recently?

Writing during an era of largely judgmental and "one side or the other" views of the Indian wars, neither Sandoz nor West can be faulted for their interpretations, omissions, and conclusions, although Mari Sandoz's fictional methodology, supported by only scant documentation, must be considered suspect by professional historians.

Unfortunately, both of these chroniclers overlooked or dismissed either military records on file in the National Archives (Sandoz) or the startling revelations about the fight at Sappa Creek, testimony by Indians collected by ethnohistorian George Hyde and formulated in the then undiscovered manuscript, Life of George Bent Written from His Letters, which was taken from Hyde's correspondence with the mixed-blood Cheyenne, George Bent, parts of which are in the Coe Collection at Yale University (Sandoz and West).* In his voluminous (two-volume) work published in 1981, People of the Sacred Mountain, Cheyenne historian Father Peter John Powell contends that although it contains some contradictions, the Bent-Hyde account of the fight is the "fullest" from the Cheyennes' perspective."[17] Powell also states that "few battles fought by the People [the Cheyennes] are more controversial than this one at the Sappa."[18] Perhaps because of this continued controversy, the Sappa Creek story has recently been "rediscovered" (often inaccurately) in popular revisionist literature.

But much of the controversy and interest in the Sappa Creek story at the time it first made news was soon overshadowed by the greater intrigue of the Battle of Little Big Horn, fought only a year later. So, until recently, the

---

* A composite of many of those letters was later published as Life of George Bent Written from His Letters.

mysteries surrounding the final engagement of the Red River War have received comparatively scant attention in the scholarship of that war. This is surprising, considering the Sappa Creek fight had the longest casualty list. Some of the events of the Red River conflict, such as the fight at Adobe Walls and the actions of Colonel Ranald Mackenzie and Colonel Nelson A. Miles, are well documented. Recently, William Y. Chalfant has done a fine job reconstructing the details of the Battle of Sappa Creek and the events leading up to it. His maps and knowledge of the local geography and specific routes to the battle site are definitive. Chalfant, like West, considers the atrocity-massacre thesis but with the addition of the Bent account. He concluded, as do most serious non-Indian scholars, that based on available evidence, the atrocity-massacre thesis, although there is much to say for it from the position of Cheyenne oral tradition, is ultimately inconclusive.[19]

Despite the inconclusiveness of the atrocity-massacre thesis, that thesis persists and carries considerable weight, with some validity, in popular accounts of the Sappa Creek fight, especially when considered in terms of cause and effect. The purpose of this study is to present one historian's interpretation of the diverse body of conflicting opinion that has clouded events over the years. My goal is to consider why this contradictory evidence came to light in the first place, and to suggest explanations of why the contradictions persist. The latter consideration takes this study on the Sappa Creek Massacre beyond studies done in the past. Among the specific arguments I advance that vary from past interpretations will be that the Cheyenne version of the fight (Bent's account) goes a long way toward explaining the immediate severity of the 6th Cavalry's actions against the Indians at Sappa Creek. Advanced also will be the idea that the long-range impact of casualties inflicted by Cheyenne raiders on civilians in Kansas, particularly the so-called Lone Tree and German massacres in 1874, provided much of the emotional voltage of the Red River War.

In the age of the "new western history," in which some scholars dig deeper than ever before for the meaning of good versus evil in a search for victims and victimizers, a controversial topic like the Sappa Creek fight can serve as a case study to bring us back to a quest for understanding, rather than as sophisticated ideological propaganda for current social and political agendas. An in-depth examination of the Sappa Creek controversy, how it has been viewed over the years, and how those views have changed with evolving societal norms can more importantly illuminate how Americans since 1875 have perceived the Indian wars in general within the larger cultural construct. This "realist" perspective, although grounded in facts, assumes a degree of interpretation based on the historiography of conflicting evidence and changing viewpoints to fill in the gaps. As such, what remains a mystery about the events at Sappa Creek on that April day in 1875 can reveal almost as much about how Americans view western history and the theme of national conquest as about what we can accurately conclude from the known facts. Earlier scholars, in relation to the available literature of the Sappa Creek engagement, have previously weighed none of these concepts in depth.

The first part of this work parallels the efforts of others by outlining the events leading to the fight on Sappa Creek and details the battle itself. The second portion compares the varied sources of the Sappa Creek controversy for the purpose of illuminating the changing views and assumptions Americans have held about white-Indian relations and warfare in the West. I have endeavored to avoid as much as possible passing judgment, based on my twentieth-century values, on the basic cultural assumptions endemic to the social fabric of nineteenth-century whites and Cheyennes. Such "presentist" evaluations, I strongly contend, dilute a meaningful evaluation of the Indian-white conflict on the nineteenth-century western military frontier. Specific acts that deviate from those cultural assumptions, however, are fair game and constitute the source of much of the Sappa Creek controversy. Cultural dimensions of both societies and how they moderated conflict between the races have long interested me, and I view them with equal or greater importance than military strategies and the reconstruction of battles. Of course, I accept full responsibility for any errors contained herein.

I wish to acknowledge the state historical societies of Colorado, Kansas, and Oklahoma for their assistance in researching the Sappa Creek controversy. The Western History Department at the Denver Public Library is always vital to my efforts, as are the military record groups of the National

Introduction
___

Archives in Washington D.C. I wish to extend gratitude to the people at the Oberlin Museum in Oberlin, Kansas, and the Wray Museum in Wray, Colorado, for much useful information. A very special thanks goes to Lyn Ryder of Niwot, Colorado, for putting me on to the papers of the John German family in the Wray Museum. Thanks, of course, also go to my wife, Linda, and my son, Darren, for their continued patience with my obsessive-compulsive behavior when it comes to writing history.

Notes

1. Barry C. Johnson, "Austin Henely: Centre of the Sappa Creek Controversy," English Westerners' Brand Book 7, no. 3 (April 1965): 11.

2. National Archives Records Administration (hereafter referred to as NARA), Records of the Adjutant General's Office (hereafter referred to as AGO), RG 94, File 3490-1874, Mrs. Delia Callihan to Adjutant General's Office, August 4, 1878.

3. Report of the Secretary of War for the Year 1875, 44th Cong., 1st sess., 1876, H. Doc. 1, 90 (hereafter referred to as "Henely's Report."); AGO, Chronological List of Actions, &c., With Indians from January 15, 1837 to January, 1891. (Washington D.C.: Government Printing Office, 1891), 59.

4. Ibid.

5. Robert M. Utley, Frontier Regulars: The United States Army and the Indian, 1866–1891 (Lincoln: University of Nebraska Press, 1984), 230. Utley states that the Battle of Sappa Creek "took the lives of nearly as many Indians as all the [engagements of the Red River War] combined." See also AGO, Actions With Indians, 56–59. This official army casualty report is misleading. It does not account for Indian casualties inflicted by civilian buffalo hunters and others during encounters in which the military was not present.

6. William D. Street, "Cheyenne Indian Massacre on the Middle Fork of the Sappa," Transactions of the Kansas State Historical Society 10, no. 4 (1907–1908): 372.

7. Ibid.

8. Ibid., 368 n. 1.

9. F. M. Lockard, "The Battle of Achilles," Kansas Magazine 2, no. 1 (July 1909): 29.

10. Mari Sandoz, Cheyenne Autumn (New York: Avon Books, 1964), 123.

11. Peter John Powell, Sweet Medicine: The Continuing Role of the Sacred Arrows, the Sun Dance, and the Sacred Buffalo Hat in Northern Cheyenne History, vol. 2 (Norman: University of Oklahoma Press, 1969), 866–867.

12. Thomas E. Way, ed., Sgt. Fred Platten's Ten Years on the Trail of the Redskins (Williams, Ariz.: Williams News Press, 1959), 11–12 (hereafter referred to as "Platten's Account"). See also Dan Thrapp,

"Attack on Sappa Creek," *Frontier Times* 37, no. 1 (December-January 1963): 69. Way's editing of Platten's memoirs is not especially well done. Way, a local justice of the peace in Williams, Arizona, and not a professional historian (although he knew Platten personally), does not relate when Platten (d. 1939) wrote down his experiences in the Indian wars. Although Platten's reminiscences are told in the first person twenty years after the fact, it is quite possible that the account was taken as an informal oral history years before Way wrote the piece. It is possible the account was related to Way by Platten's widow, Mary, whom Way acknowledged in the book's Introduction as providing indispensable aid in compiling the account of Platten's army career in Kansas and Arizona. Of course, the possibility exists that Way embellished Platten's stories to increase reader interest.

13. Gene Jones, "Curse of Ta-Kanah," *Real West* 6, no. 29 (May 1963): 49–50.

14. G. Derek West, "The Battle of Sappa Creek, 1875," *Kansas Historical Quarterly* 34, no. 2 (summer 1968): 168.

15. Ibid.

16. Ibid.

17. Peter John Powell, *People of the Sacred Mountain: A History of the Northern Cheyenne Chiefs and Warrior Societies, 1830–1879, With an Epilog, 1969–1974*, 2 vols. (San Francisco: Harper & Row, 1981), 2:1357 n. 7.

18. Ibid.

19. William Y. Chalfant, *Cheyennes at Dark Water Creek: The Last Fight of the Red River War* (Norman: University of Oklahoma Press, 1997).

Massacre at Cheyenne Hole

Chapter I

Background: The Buffalo War

Buffalo Bill, Buffalo Bill,
Never missed and never will;
Always aims and shoots to kill
And the company pays his buffalo bill

—Anonymous, circa 1875

About noon on a hot June day somewhere in the vastness of the unbroken southern plains during the early 1870s, an obscure event took place, one of many similar events that collectively marked the beginning of the end of Indian independence on the western plains. On that day a hide man named John Cook carefully studied a herd of about 1,000 buffalo. "I now had what I had so often heard about but had never actually seen before," Cook remembered, "*a stand.*" From a concealed position close to the herd, Cook shot the lead bull and the slaughter began. "After I had killed twenty-five that I knew of," Cook recalled, "the smoke from my gun commenced to hang low, and was slow in disappearing. So I shifted my position and in doing so, [I] got still closer."

An hour or so later, after changing guns because the first weapon grew too hot to handle, John Cook fired at a large bull, breaking one of its legs but failing to bring the beast down. The wounded creature hopped around frantically, its disabled leg flopping back and forth, useless. The bull crashed into several other animals in the herd, then panicked and ran as well as it could through the center of the remaining buffalo. Its frenzied actions threw the remainder of the herd into a state of panic. The buffalo stampeded. The stand was broken. Cook pursued them on foot, firing as rapidly as he could as long as there were animals within rifle range:

> I moved up to a dead buffalo and got in several good shots . . . I moved again, on through the dead ones . . . and fired three more shots and quit. As I walked back through where the carcasses lay the thickest, I could not help but think that I had done wrong to make such a slaughter for the hides alone . . . In counting them just as they lay there, their eyes glassy in death, [I found] I had killed eighty-eight; and several left the ground with more bad than slight wounds.[1]

Other hunters bettered Cook's record with stands of their own.

Wright Mooar	96
Kirk Jordan	100
Charles Rath	107
Vic Smith	107
Doc Zahl	120
Tom Nixon	204
Orlando A. Bond	250[2]

These scenes of slaughter followed the discovery in 1870 that buffalo hides could be tanned to make fine leather. The demand for hides skyrocketed both in the United States and in Europe, and the buffalo hunters responded to the need. Collectively, their activities helped precipitate the Red River War with the southern plains tribes. That war would conclude in mystery and controversy in 1875 at Sappa Creek.[3]

With the escalating demand for hides in eastern tanneries, the new town of Dodge City, Kansas (originally called Buffalo City), about midway on the buffalo ranges of the southern plains, became the commercial and outfitting center of the new big business in buffalo hides. In September 1872 the

Santa Fe Railroad reached Dodge City. In the three months that followed, the railroad shipped 43,029 buffalo hides east. During the next three years, the Santa Fe Railroad shipped an estimated total of 1,378,359 hides to eastern tanneries. Companies east and west incorporated to facilitate all aspects of the hide business.[4]

Firearms manufacturers met the demand for better and more powerful long-range rifles to bring down the shaggy beasts. Remington responded with a "rolling-block" breech-loading rifle using up to .44-90 bottleneck caliber cartridges. The special cartridges for Remington's buffalo rifles soon were being produced in .50-70 caliber. Sharps met the call with an octagon-shaped barreled rifle up to 50 inches long and firing a .50 caliber cartridge that used 380 grains of lead and burned 120 grains of powder. The gun came complete with a portable reloading kit, including a lead mold with which to make bullets on the range. When the big weapons proved insufficient due to wind resistance on the plains, the manufacturers modified them and sent test models to the buffalo hunters for evaluation. By 1883, throughout all the ranges of the Great Plains, the American bison, which had numbered in the millions, came near to extinction.[5]

The efficiency of "the stand" John Cook enjoyed meant that skinners, who followed the hunters, could do their work more quickly than if the carcasses were strewn over the prairie for miles, as would have been the case in a more sporting "chase" from horseback. Most hunters knew it would be wasteful to kill more buffalo than their skinners could handle in a day, but as one veteran hide man, Frank Mayer, later claimed, it was not the waste of buffalo that restrained a hunter on the stand. Hunters simply did not want to squander expensive ammunition.[6]

Despite predictions to the contrary, many hunters apparently could not foresee an end to the buffalo. But augmented by the spread of bovine disease, herd separation by the transcontinental railroad, and pot hunting by homesteaders, the end came swiftly. Writing home to relatives from Salina, Kansas, in 1860, an early hunter, James R. Mead, one of the founders of Wichita, stated: "There is no danger of them all being killed for some time to come, not a bit. They are like the locusts of Egypt."[7] Twenty years later the buffalo were, for all practical purposes, extinct in Kansas. Writing his memoirs in the 1890s, Mead lamented the swiftness with which the slaughter of the buffalo occurred and how it changed the environment forever:

> The beauties and blessings of civilization are very largely a myth . . . The freedom and beauty and the chivalry of the plains are a thing of the past; nothing now remains but dull, plodding labor, and many thousands of settlers are now squatted down on a little circumscribed piece of prairie land, trying to eke out an existence . . . All these changes which have taken place during the last thirty years seem like a dream as my mind travels back over the events that have occurred during this period of my life . . . In those happy days the plains rejoiced in their pristine beauty, unmarred by civilization, which first destroys . . . what Providence placed here for man's use, and then commences the slow process of reproducing what it has destroyed. Then these plains were covered with unnumbered myriad's [sic] of buffalo, sufficient to supply the nation with meat. The wanton greed of the white man has slaughtered the last one. The elk, the deer, and the antelope have likewise disappeared.[8]

Even in the 1890s, men like James Mead could grasp the irreversible tragedy of upsetting ecological balances by eliminating a species like the American bison. "The buffalo, the gray wolves, and the ravens—companions in life—mingled their bones when swift destruction overtook them," he wrote.

> The buffalo were killed by the bullets of hunters, the wolves were killed with strychnine for their furs, and the ravens died from eating the poisoned carcasses of both, so that they became practically extinct about the same time. The prairie dogs also disappeared over the larger part of the buffalo range, but they died from natural causes, as they are not able to live in a country which is not trampled bare and eaten down close to the ground by [other] animals. In other words, wherever the buffalo ceased to eat, the prairie grass and the rank grass grew up, and the prairie dogs [and other species] perished.[9]

Almost perishing too in the wake of this upheaval were the traditional cultures of the southern plains tribes.

4

In all likelihood, the near extinction of the buffalo herds of the plains could not have been accomplished without the support of the U.S. Army. By eliminating the buffalo, Euro-American civilization could undermine the economy and traditional way of life of the Plains Indians, freeing up agricultural land for white settlers. Indians were impoverished in the process and forced to remain on reservations and endure a way of life they did not choose.

In the 1870s, Major General Philip Sheridan, the commander of the Division of the Missouri, which included the Great Plains, gave his whole-hearted approval to the buffalo slaughter. Sheridan proposed, as he had done in Virginia's Shenandoah Valley during the Civil War, to initiate a policy of total war against recalcitrant Indians who refused to submit to reservation life. Sheridan believed that so long as the buffalo remained, men would leave the reservation to seek them out.

Sheridan's policy, of course, can be viewed as a kind of cultural genocide. In 1875, when the state legislature of Texas considered a bill to protect the depleted buffalo within the state's borders, Sheridan objected. Instead of extending protection, the general believed, the Texas legislature should strike a bronze medal with a dead buffalo on one side and a discouraged Indian on the other and bestow it on the buffalo hunters. He saw the hide men as forerunners of civilization. "These men have done in the last two years, and will do more in the next years, to settle the vexed Indian question, than the entire regular army has done in the last thirty years," Sheridan proclaimed in a frequently quoted statement. He went on to urge the legislature to send lead and powder to the buffalo hunters, allowing them to "kill, skin, and sell until the buffaloes are exterminated." With their economic base destroyed, the plains tribes would have little choice but to return to the reservation, segregating themselves from white settlers, a condition Sheridan believed would lead to lasting peace on the frontier.[10]

According to stipulations agreed to by peace chiefs and other warriors of the Cheyennes, Arapahos, Kiowas, Comanches, and plains Apaches in the Treaties of Medicine Lodge that concluded in 1867, Indian hunters were not to pursue the buffalo north of the Arkansas River in southeastern

Colorado Territory and southwestern Kansas. In return, the tribes received reservations south of the Arkansas in Indian Territory.[*][11] With the increase in the hide trade after 1870, many of the buffalo that were not slaughtered on Kansas prairies migrated southward into Indian Territory and the Texas Panhandle, mingling with herds already in those areas and escaping hunting pressure from the hide men. The buffalo hunters were not supposed to cross south of the Arkansas onto the lands reserved to the tribes, but after 1874, when the bison became scarce on legal hunting grounds, the hunters came anyway, claiming a hunting boundary line south to the Cimarron River, and then even farther south and west into Texas.[12] When the slaughter began there, sometimes almost within sight of Indian villages, the tribes naturally objected. "They [the buffalo] are our cattle, our money," an unidentified chief said. "Why do you wish to destroy them? They are all we possess."[13]

On the central southern plains, one of the most important tribes to have engaged in continual warfare over the years with whites were the Cheyennes. Few, if any other tribes fared worse than the Cheyennes for their militant opposition to the white settlers' westward expansion during the nineteenth century. The Cheyennes called themselves *Tsis tsis tas*, meaning "People alike" or simply "the People."[14] They originally came from the north and east, from the lands that became Minnesota, pushing onto the Great Plains along with their allies the Arapahos in response to pressure from enemies. The Lakotas gave this Algonquian linguistic group the name *Shai ena*, which means "people speaking a strange tongue." Whites transliterated this name to "Cheyenne."[15] As a migrant people, the Cheyennes fought many wars with other tribes before settling in lands east of the Rocky Mountains. After acquiring the horse from neighboring tribes, the Cheyennes later formed powerful alliances with these tribes to help resist the whites.

---

[*] The Medicine Lodge treaties, which concluded near a stream of the same name in southwest Kansas in 1867, were evidence of the intention of white society to dominate the Great Plains and everything on them. The treaties represented a major attempt to segregate the plains tribes on reservations for the purpose of phasing out their traditional cultures and acculturating them to Euro-American society.

In 1780 the Cheyennes numbered about 3,500. During the period of the fur trade in the 1830s and 1840s the Cheyennes began dividing into two distinct geographical groups. The Northern Cheyennes remained in lands that would become the Dakotas, Wyoming, and Montana. There they closely allied themselves with the Lakotas. A southern group, attracted by trade at Bent's Fort, took hold of lands between the Platte and Arkansas Rivers in an area that would one day become portions of Kansas and Colorado. There they became middlemen in an elaborate system of trade with other tribes for the north and south. In their trade, warfare, and on buffalo hunts, the Cheyennes wandered far from these lands, and the northern and southern groups frequently made long journeys to visit each other.

But in 1830 or possibly 1833 and again about 1872, disaster struck the Cheyennes. Both events involved the desecration of sacred tribal possessions so revered by the Cheyennes that the tribe's spiritual unity was affected. After these disasters the power and independence of the Cheyennes declined as they suffered continued calamities.

The first tragedy was the capture by Pawnees of Maahotse, the Sacred Arrows, from which flowed the energy of Maheo, the creator himself, to the People in their everyday lives. "Some of the old people say that this was in 1830," George Bent remembered, "but most of them say it was in 1833, the year the stars fell.* The great meteor shower came in November and all the Indians thought the world was coming to an end. The dogs collected in bands and howled like wolves, the women and children wailed, and the warriors mounted their war horses and rode about, singing their death songs."[16]

In the years to follow, the Cheyennes suffered as never before. A cholera epidemic brought by white emigrants over the Oregon Trail spread to the Cheyennes after 1849, killing hundreds. A decade later the Colorado gold rush and the founding of Denver City displaced the Cheyennes from prime winter buffalo ranges and the Treaty of Fort Wise restricted them to a small region in southeast Colorado Territory.

---

* The Leonid meteor shower of November 14, 1833.

Conflicts with whites along the South Platte and Smoky Hill Trails led to bloodshed and war in 1864. In November of that year the village of the peace chief Black Kettle was attacked by detachments of Colorado territorial volunteers under Colonel John M. Chivington, an ordained Methodist minister. Many women and children were butchered in the attack, which came to be called the Sand Creek Massacre.[17] "After the massacre, other Cheyennes who had been on the Arkansas River came over to Sand Creek," remembered Cheyenne oral historian John Stands in Timber. "My grandmother was with that party. None of them ever forgot what they saw there."[18] Chivington's brutal attack unleashed retribution by the Cheyennes, especially the Dog Soldiers, one of the most independent of the tribe's military societies. Even when a peace commission from Washington secured the Treaty of the Little Arkansas in 1865, whereby most of the Southern Cheyennes agreed to a reservation south of the Arkansas, the Dog Soldiers swore never to surrender their lands in the Smoky Hill and Republican valleys.*

Hundreds of whites poured into those lands during the post–Civil War years of the 1860s, taking homesteads on the prime Kansas buffalo ranges. With the Cheyennes south of the Arkansas the buffalo concentrated in the ceded lands, where white settlers hunted them for food. This cultural displacement was too much for many Cheyennes, who began raiding the white settlements in Kansas during 1867 and 1868. Again in 1867, at the great councils of Medicine Lodge, the Cheyennes, including the usually militant Dog Soldiers, agreed to another reservation in Indian Territory. But again many young warriors, for various reasons, ultimately refused to abide by the new treaty and began raiding the settlements, stage stations, and construction sites along the Union Pacific and Union Pacific Eastern Division

---

* The promised reservation did not materialize before war broke out again. Congress, preoccupied with Reconstruction in the defeated South, did not even ratify the treaty until 1866. By 1867 war had broken out again as a result of a heavy handed council between Dog Soldier chiefs and Major General Winfield Scott Hancock, commander of the Department of the Missouri. Hancock precipitated war by burning a Dog Soldier village near Fort Larned, Kansas, because the Indians, fearful of treachery as had occurred at Sand Creek, deserted the village rather than treat with Hancock.

(Kansas Pacific in 1869) railroads making their way across the central plains in 1868. A number of whites were ruthlessly murdered during the raids of 1867–1868.[19]

In retaliation, Major General Philip Sheridan unleashed the first of several actions aimed at total war against the Cheyennes. In November of 1868 Lieutenant Colonel George Armstrong Custer and the 7th Cavalry smashed Black Kettle's village of Southern Cheyennes on the Washita River in Indian Territory. Some, but not all, of the warriors in Black Kettle's camp had been raiding the white settlements the previous summer. The devastating winter campaign was a crushing defeat for the Cheyennes. In the attack Custer's soldiers killed the peace chief Black Kettle.[20]

During the summer of 1869 Sheridan ordered the Republican River Expedition, consisting of elements of the 4th and 10th Cavalry regiments, to hunt down the Dog Soldiers under Tall Bull, who had not been present during Custer's attack at Washita. The command under Major Eugene A. Carr, a Medal of Honor winner, along with Frank North's famed Pawnee Scouts, caught the Dog Soldiers by surprise at a place called Summit Springs in Colorado Territory. Tall Bull died at Summit Springs along with many of his warriors. Never again did the Dog Soldiers pose a formidable independent military threat to westward expansion. With the decisive Battle of Summit Springs the southern Cheyennes finally settled on their Indian Territory reservation on the Canadian River.[21]

Then in about 1872, *Esevone*, the Sacred Buffalo Hat, through which *Maheo* himself pours life into the lives of Cheyenne women and makes them fruitful, was desecrated by a Cheyenne woman. The wife of the temporary hat keeper ripped a horn off of the sacred headpiece in a fit of anger. Although Esevone resided with the northern people, it had been especially sacred to the Suhtai, being given to them even before the once distinct Suhtai joined the Cheyennes as one of their bands. The Cheyennes came to believe that *Esevone*'s desecration affected both northern and southern people alike.[22] Soon afterward the Southern Cheyennes witnessed the trespass into their reserved lands by the Kansas buffalo hunters. The illegal slaughter perpetuated by these hunters, combined with general impoverishment on the reservation, led some of the southern people to resist the whites one last time. Joining forces with the Kiowas and Comanches in the Red River War, the remnants of a once imposing military force of Southern Cheyennes would take the field of battle for the last time in a desperate attempt to preserve what was left of their traditional culture. That free and unrestricted way of life would finally come to an end on a blustery April day in the old hunting grounds of the Dog Soldiers along the banks of Sappa Creek.[23]

Notes

1. John R. Cook, *The Border and the Buffalo: The Untold Story of the Southwest Plains* (Topeka, Kans.: Crane and Co., 1907), 150–152.

2. Tom McHugh, *The Time of the Buffalo* (Lincoln: University of Nebraska Press, 1979), 261. Hugh describes another stand in which Tom Nixon set a record by killing 120 buffalo in twenty minutes. The slaughter overheated his rifle so that it was ruined at the end of the "hunt."

3. David A. Dary, *The Buffalo Book: The Saga of an American Symbol* (New York: Avon Books, 1974), 94. See also David D. Smits, "The Frontier Army and the Destruction of the Buffalo, 1865–1883," *Western History Quarterly* 25, no. 3, (autumn 1994): 313–338.

4. Ibid., 96.

5. Ibid., 100.

6. McHugh, *Time of the Buffalo*, 261.

7. James R. Mead, *Hunting and Trading on the Great Plains, 1859–1875* (Norman: University of Oklahoma Press, 1986), 82.

8. Ibid., 256–257.

9. Ibid., 74.

10. Cook, *The Border and the Buffalo*, 163–164. For an excellent analysis of Sheridan's views on total war see Paul A. Hutton, "Phil Sheridan's Frontier," *Montana: The Magazine of Western History* 38, no.1 (winter 1988): 16–31. The best Sheridan biography is Paul A. Hutton, *Phil Sheridan and His Army* (Lincoln: University of Nebraska Press, 1985).

11. For the Medicine Lodge treaties see Douglas C. Jones, *The Treaty of Medicine Lodge* (Norman: University of Oklahoma Press, 1966).

12. George Bird Grinnell, *The Fighting Cheyennes* (Norman: University of Oklahoma Press, 1956), 321.

13. W. S. Nye, *Carbine & Lance: The Story of Old Fort Sill* (Norman: University of Oklahoma Press, 1937), 187.

14. George E. Hyde, *Life of George Bent Written from His Letters* (Norman: University of Oklahoma Press, 1968), 3.

15. Ibid.

16. Hyde, *Life of George Bent*, 51.

17. For the Sand Creek Massacre see Stan Hoig, *The Sand Creek Massacre* (Norman: University of Oklahoma Press, 1964).

18. John Stands in Timber and Margot Liberty, *Cheyenne Memories* (New Haven: Yale University Press, 1967), 170.

19. For the warfare between Cheyennes and whites between 1867 and 1869 see John H. Monnett, *The Battle of Beecher Island and the Indian War of 1868–1869* (Niwot: University Press of Colorado, 1992).

20. For the Battle of the Washita see Stan Hoig, *The Battle of the Washita* (Lincoln: University of Nebraska Press, 1976).

21. For Summit Springs see James T. King, *War Eagle: A Life of General Eugene A. Carr* (Lincoln: University of Nebraska Press, 1963).

22. Powell, *People of the Sacred Mountain*, 1:xvii–xviii.

23. It is beyond the scope of the current study to examine in depth the history, culture, and spiritual beliefs of the Cheyenne tribe prior to the Red River War. Fortunately, we are blessed with fine material compiled over the years on these subjects. One of the most complete secondary sources is the two-volume history by Father Peter John Powell, *People of the Sacred Mountain*. See also Grinnell, *The Fighting Cheyennes*, and Donald J. Berthrong, *The Southern Cheyennes* (Norman: University of Oklahoma Press, 1963). More cutting-edge studies on Cheyenne culture include George A. Dorsey, *The Cheyennes*, 2 vols. (Chicago: Field Columbian Museum, 1905); E. Adamson Hoebel, *The Cheyennes: Indians of the Great Plains* (New York: Holt, Rinehart and Winston, 1960); and K. N. Llewellyn and E. Adamson Hoebel, *The Cheyenne Way: Conflict and Case Law in Primitive Jurisprudence* (Norman: University of Oklahoma Press, 1941).

———

Chapter II

Prelude: Adobe Walls and After

> Now there was at this time a new leader among the Quahadi Comanches whose name was Isatai. He was bulletproof. Isatai promised to protect all Indians who believed in him. To prove this he vomited up a wagonload of rifle cartridges. There were witnesses who said they saw him do so. He told the Indians he could produce endless cartridges and that they too would be bulletproof before the soldier guns.
>
> —a popular paraphrase of ethnologist James Mooney, 1890s

Years before the whites came to the lands of the people but after the Cheyennes had migrated onto the Great Plains, *Maheo*, the creator of all, revealed himself to a mortal. The revelation took place inside a cave located on what afterward was known as *Noahavose*, the Sacred Mountain,* which rises near the modern town of Sturgis, South Dakota. There *Maheo* gave to Sweet Medicine, the great prophet and culture hero of the Cheyennes, *Maahotse*, the four Sacred Arrows through which *Maheo* pours his divine life into the lives of the People, especially the warriors. Throughout the remaining years of his life Sweet Medicine taught the word of *Maheo* to the Cheyennes.

———

* Known today as Bear Butte because the mountain resembles a sleeping grizzly bear.

One day, years after the revelation to Sweet Medicine, when the tribe was still together living on the northern plains, the People were camped in a big village near Devil's Tower in present-day Wyoming. Sweet Medicine called together the military societies and ordered them to build him a lodge of cedar poles covered with rye grass and cottonwood bark. Sweet Medicine knew his time had come. This was his death lodge. He then ordered the village to be moved so that he could be alone when he died. After the new village was set up, Sweet Medicine sent word for the People to return and hear his last words to them. When they had come he began to speak.

"My friends," he said according to oral tradition,

> Once I was young and able, but a man lives only a short time, and now I am old and helpless and ready to leave you. I have brought you many things, sent by the gods for your use. You live the way I have taught you, and follow the laws. You must not forget them, for they have given you strength and the ability to support yourselves and your families.
>
> There is a time coming, though, when many things will change. Strangers called Earth men will appear among you. Their skins are light-colored, and their ways are powerful. They clip their hair short and speak no Indian tongue. Follow nothing that these Earth Men do, but keep your own ways that I have taught you as long as you can.
>
> The buffalo will disappear, at last, and another animal will take its place, a slick animal with a long tail and split hoofs, whose flesh you will learn to eat . . . Remember what I have said.
>
> But at last you will not remember. Your ways will change. You will leave your religion for something new. You will lose respect for your leaders and start quarreling with one another. You will lose track of your relations and marry women from your own families. You will take after the Earth Men's ways and forget good things by which you have lived and in the end become worse than crazy.
>
> I am sorry to say these things, but I have seen them, and you will find that they come true.[1]

Then the People fell silent, contemplating what Sweet Medicine had told them. But, at last, they did not believe him. Finally they went away, leaving him there alone. He was never seen again.

By the early 1870s, much of what Sweet Medicine told the Cheyennes had come true. The plains were being swept clean of buffalo to make room for herds of longhorn cattle already being driven north from Texas along the Chisholm Trail through the lands of the southern people to be loaded on the boxcars of the Kansas Pacific Railroad at Abilene, Kansas. Other herds came up the Goodnight-Loving Trail to Denver and present-day Cheyenne. What was left the cattlemen sold to the Indian reservations for beef rations. Soon the buffalo would be gone altogether and the Indians would become completely dependent upon the distasteful fat beef of the white man.

The slaughter of the buffalo was only one of several mounting pressures and strictures of reservation life that helped edge the Southern Cheyennes toward war during the winter and spring of 1873–1874. According to the Treaty of Medicine Lodge signed in 1867, the Cheyennes "accepted" a reservation in the western portion of Indian Territory. After the Battle of Summit Springs in 1869, which broke the power of the Dog Soldier military society, most of the southern people settled on this reservation. At first they drew their rations and annuities near Camp Supply, but in 1870 their agency was moved to a new site 100 miles down the North Canadian River, where in 1874 Fort Reno was built. South of the Cheyenne-Arapaho lands was the reservation of the Comanches and Kiowas, augmented by Fort Sill.

Overseeing the reservations as part of President Grant's Peace Policy, which was intended to purify the government Indian Bureau of corruption, were agents nominated by the Society of Friends, which had gained the president's ear in respect to Indian affairs. From offices in Lawrence, Kansas, the Central Superintendency (covering Kansas and Indian Territory) was headed by Superintendent Enoch Hoag, described as a pious visionary, and his clerk, Cyrus Beede, whom General Philip Sheridan once described as "a little too simple for this earth."[2] The Quakers appointed the elderly Brinton Darlington agent for the Cheyennes and Arapahos. In 1870, upon Darlington's death, the able John D. Miles became agent. Pacifism informed Quaker methods for handling their Indian wards.

Frequently young Comanche and Kiowa warriors left their reservation and rode west into the Texas Panhandle to make raids on white settlements. A few young Cheyennes joined these men in the raids. But overall, before

1874, the Cheyennes remained on the reservation (Darlington Agency), where they fell prey to poverty and whiskey peddlers, who swarmed over the Kansas border to ply their trade among the Indians.

According to the Peace Policy, U.S. troops stationed on the reservations were under the authority of the agents, whereas troops in Texas could not pursue raiders back across the Red River, the border between Texas and Indian Territory, and onto the reservations. Accordingly, Fort Sill became a "city of refuge" for the raiders, who would legally receive government rations, supplies, and protection there while resting between raids. The only measure the military could legally take was to bolster the Texas defenses when General Sherman realigned the Department of Texas under Sheridan's Division of the Missouri, giving the command to General Christopher C. Augur and extending the authority of the department to include Fort Sill.[3]

By the winter of 1873–1874, the manifestations of Esevone's mutilation became more apparent to the Southern Cheyennes. From out of the Sangre de Cristo Range in the Rockies, deadly blizzards repeatedly and furiously swept south that winter across the Texas Panhandle and onto the reservation, leaving the prairie grass covered with a blanket of snow and ice. With the buffalo herds more than 100 miles to the west in Texas, too far for hunting parties to travel through the blizzards and heavy snow cover, many of the People began to starve. Some butchered their emaciated horses for food.[4]

As the bitter cold continued on into early spring on the fronts of repeated storms, many of the chiefs and warrior society leaders, who had been too proud to accept the white man's beef, began showing up at the Darlington Agency to receive rations. Eagle Head, Old Whirlwind, and White Shield brought in 140 lodges. Grey Beard's Suhtai and Heap of Birds came in, as well as White Horse, burdened with sick women and children and elderly people. This was the first time the Dog Soldier chief White Horse, who had survived such battles as Beecher Island and Summit Springs, had asked the whites for food.[5] People of the Great Plains today, like non-Indians in 1874, often have trouble imagining what must have gone through the minds of the Cheyennes, with their remarkable assumptions regarding natural balances and rhythms, when they witnessed firsthand the rapid and devastating changes in the prairie ecology during the 1870s.

To make matters worse, during the early spring of 1874 white horse thieves operating out of Kansas, and a problem since the creation of the reservation, stepped up their raids of Cheyenne pony herds in Indian Territory. First they stole George Bent's herd and drove them to the Big Bend of the Arkansas, a noted hideout for horse thieves. About March 11, 1874, William "Hurricane Bill" Martin, one of the most notorious of the Kansas robbers, stole forty-three of the best ponies from Little Robe's camp. Shortly thereafter some whites reported these horses being offered for sale in Dodge City. The army did nothing about the incident, and the Cheyenne chiefs told Agent Miles that if Little Robe's stock were not recovered they would not be able to prevent their young men from raiding the Kansas settlements in retaliation.[6]

In May the chiefs' predictions came true. A party of warriors set out to seek repayment for Little Robe's stolen horses. Among them was Little Robe's son, Sitting Medicine. The Indians struck near Sun City, Kansas, where they captured horses, mules, and cattle from white settlers. Before the war party could escape back across the Kansas state line to the safety of the reservation, troopers of the 6th Cavalry pursued and fired on them. To make matters worse, rumors spread throughout some of the outlying camps on the reservation that the soldiers had killed Sitting Medicine in the engagement. Thus small war parties of Cheyennes set out to avenge the death of Little Robe's son. They killed at least one white civilian before they returned to their camps.[7]

But of all the grievances and misery afflicting the southern people that year, the worst remained the ubiquitous buffalo hunters.[8] In one terrible summer of slaughter in 1872, the hide men drastically reduced the numbers of buffalo in southern Kansas. The next year, in direct violation of the Treaty of Medicine Lodge, the white hunters moved southward across the Kansas state line and into Indian Territory to slaughter the herds along the Cimarron River. Soldiers who were supposed to patrol the border and turn back poachers ignored the hunters slipping onto the Indian lands. The sooner the buffalo were exterminated, the sooner the Indians would lose their reason for roaming over the prairie.[9]

In 1873 the slaughter in the Cimarron Valley was so extensive that the once enormous southern herd would never again migrate that far north.

Instead, the buffalo would halt their northern progress along the banks of the Canadian River.[10] During the years 1872 and 1873, an estimated 7.5 million buffalo were butchered on the southern plains by the white hide hunters.[11]

With the buffalo wiped out south of the Cimarron, the dawn of the new year in 1874 found the hide men making plans to take the hunt even farther south in the Texas Panhandle—on the Canadian River, adjacent to the Indian reservations. Technically, they would not be trespassing on the reservation lands. But technicalities meant little to the Southern Cheyennes and their allies. As far as they were concerned, the white peace commissioners had promised at the time of the Medicine Lodge treaties that all the buffalo south of the Arkansas would be reserved for the Indians alone to hunt.[12]

The Indians believed Major Richard Irving Dodge, the commander of Fort Dodge, Kansas, was supposed to protect "their" buffalo from the poachers. But when a delegation of hunters led by Wright Mooar and Steele Frazier inquired of Dodge what the government's attitude toward their presence along the Canadian might be, Dodge, although evasive in his deliberation, gave them the go-ahead: "Boys," he exclaimed, "If I were a buffalo hunter, I would hunt where the buffaloes are."[13] When Comanches brought word to the Southern Cheyennes, Arapahos, and Kiowas that hide men had been spotted in the Canadian River country, many of the warriors, both young and old, prepared for one last war with the whites.

With Major Dodge's support, the hide hunters finalized plans to hold the 1874 buffalo hunt on the Staked Plains, 150 miles south of Dodge City. Billy Dixon led the hunting caravan that spring. At twenty-four, Dixon was already a seasoned hide hunter. With him were some forty-nine other men, including Bat Masterson, a year-and-a-half veteran of the hide trade.[14]

The whites set up a base near the old ruins of the abandoned trading post called Adobe Walls, established in the 1840s by the fur trading cartel of Bent, St. Vrain and Company in a futile attempt to establish trade with the Comanches and Kiowas. The ruins had been the site of Kit Carson's fight with Comanches in 1864. Soon the hide men built a row of sod-and-log buildings near the crumbling ruins. By May 1874, some 200 hide men were operating out of the tiny settlement, also known as Adobe Walls.[15]

The summer of 1874 came late, as had the spring, delaying the northward migration of the buffalo. But when the beasts did eventually come north, the hide men from Adobe Walls slaughtered them by the thousands. After skinning off the robes, the glistening carcasses of the animals were left on the prairie to rot in the sun. Comanche wolves (scouts) brought word to the reservations of the immense slaughter. Soon many of the Southern Cheyennes cast their lot for war along with the Comanches and Kiowas and pledged to wipe out the whites at Adobe Walls.[16]

That spring a new leader arose among the Quahadi Comanches. His name was Isatai, "Wolf Droppings." He claimed to possess the powers of a holy man and declared that he was bulletproof. At a Sun Dance, Isatai convinced the Comanches, including the young mixed-blood war leader, Quanah Parker, that his medicine would protect them if they moved to attack the hide men at Adobe Walls. "Go ahead," Isatai told the warriors in the Sun Dance camp, "those white men can't shoot you. With my medicine I will stop their guns. When you charge, you will wipe them all out."[17] Soon many of the Cheyenne warriors, including remnants of the old Dog Soldier warrior society, fell under Isatai's spell and left the reservation with Quanah and his Comanche followers to attack the whites at Adobe Walls.

Near dawn on June 17, 1874, the combined force of warriors formed a battle line atop a bluff nearby the village of Adobe Walls. Isatai was with them, astride his horse, intently surveying the rude settlement. He was naked except for a headdress made of sage stems, and his body was covered with yellow paint. The warriors charged and drove off the whites' horses, picketed outside the settlement walls. But the Indians had not caught the hide men by surprise. During the night, inside Hanrahan's Saloon in the center of the small community, the cracking of a ridgepole under the weight of heavy sod had awakened many of the whites. They were busy repairing the damaged building when the Indians appeared. The whites were heavily armed with their .50 caliber buffalo guns. Barricading themselves inside the log-and-sod buildings, they were ready for the attack.

The Comanches swept in first, mounted on swift ponies, followed by the Cheyennes and fighting men of other tribes who had joined the crusade against the buffalo hunters. Some of the warriors pulled up their horses and made insulting gestures at the whites inside the buildings. Others dismounted and took cover behind the scattered wagons outside the settlement. Still others came charging in at full speed, firing from under the necks of their warhorses. Comanche warriors killed two whites early in the fight, Ike and "Shorty" Shadler, whom the attacking Indians caught outside the walls. Isatai did not take part in the charge. Instead he watched the fighting intently from the safety of a nearby hill.

Soon things went bad for the Indians, as the long-range buffalo guns took their toll. A number of warriors charged right up to the walls of the buildings in which the buffalo hunters were barricaded. The Cheyenne fighting man Horse Road, who had already taken one bullet, rode up to the door of one of the buildings and began beating on it with the butt of his rifle in an attempt to break it in. But the heavy door held, and Horse Road was shot to pieces as he tried to break the door down.

During the thick of the battle, Quanah and another Comanche jumped on the roof of one of the buildings, where they poked holes in the sod roof and began firing on the whites inside. But soon they were caught in a dangerous cross fire and quickly had to abandon their exposed position. Not long thereafter, a bullet caught Quanah in the side, severely wounding the Comanche war leader. Quanah was out of the fighting.

The assault continued throughout the morning hours. Warriors charged the settlement, circled around it, fell back, regrouped, and charged again. Each attack was accompanied by the sound of bugle calls that, some of the whites claimed, were made by a black trooper of the 10th Cavalry who had deserted and joined the Comanches. By noon the charges slackened, for it had become apparent to most of the warriors that Isatai was a fool and his medicine was worthless. By early afternoon the Indians withdrew completely.[18]

Inside the buildings, Billy Dixon, Bat Masterson, and the other terrified buffalo hunters were greatly relieved they had survived. "I could never see how we escaped," Billy Dixon remembered years later, "for at times the bullets poured in like hail and made us hug the sod walls like gophers when a hawk is swooping past . . . [and the] bullets rattled round us like hail."[19]

Isatai claimed that his medicine would have worked and the whites wiped out had not one of the Cheyennes that morning killed a skunk on the way to attack Adobe Walls. The killing of the skunk, Isatai claimed, had broken his medicine and resulted in the Indians' defeat. Filled with anger, the Cheyennes drew up their horses close to Isatai and shouted with rage and contempt: "What's the matter with your medicine? You got skunk medicine!" That day at Adobe Walls, Isatai was disgraced for life.[20]

The Cheyennes claimed six warriors killed at Adobe Walls. They were Horse Road (Horse Chief), Stone Teeth, Coyote, Spotted Feathers (Spots on Feathers), Stone Calf's son, and Walks on the Ground. Six Comanches were killed.[21] To make matters worse nine of the warriors, among them Horse Road, had been killed so close to the whites' guns that it was impossible to recover their bodies to bury them as brave men who had died a warrior's death. Soon after the Battle of Adobe Walls, however, a party of Cheyennes led by Prairie Chief returned to Adobe Walls to recover the bodies of Horse Road and the others who had been slain. The white hide hunters had abandoned the settlement. One of the members of the burial party, Thunder Cloud or Thunder Bird, described years later what the Cheyennes found. "When we came back [to Adobe Walls] four months later," he remembered, "we found that the hunters had cut off the heads of our [dead] warriors and put them up on poles before they abandoned the place. We then burned it to the ground."[22]

After Adobe Walls the warriors—Cheyennes, Comanches, Kiowas, and Plains Apaches—took their revenge on settlers and travelers in Kansas and Texas. In July 1874, General Sherman ratified a state of war with the southern tribes—the Red River War. The order recorded the failed policy of separating military and civil authority at the reservation line. No longer would the southern reservations provide refuge for warriors returning from raids. After July, U.S. troops were turned loose to pursue warriors no matter where they might flee. But the new policy resurrected an old problem: how to distinguish Indians who had been committing depredations from those who wished to remain at peace.[23]

For the commander of the Division of the Missouri, General Philip Sheridan, the strategy of the Red River War would closely parallel that of his campaign against the Southern Cheyennes in 1868–1869, with the exception that operations would commence during the summer months. Columns of troops would converge on the Indians in the Texas Panhandle and wear them down, thus hastening their return to the reservations. Operating southward out of Fort Dodge within the military Department of the Missouri were eight companies of the 6th Cavalry and four companies of the 5th Infantry under Colonel Nelson A. Miles, destined in the Red River War to inaugurate a career as one of the very few successful Indian-fighting generals.

Four companies of the 8th Cavalry under Major William R. Price pushed eastward. Meanwhile, the Buffalo soldiers of the 10th Cavalry, under Lieutenant Colonel John W. Davidson, moved directly west from Fort Sill. Moving northward, strike forces under Lieutenant Colonel George P. Buell, 11th Infantry, and eight companies of the 4th Cavalry under Colonel Ranald S. Mackenzie completed the envelopment. Sheridan ordered friendly Indians to be enrolled at the agencies and to be accounted for frequently. At Darlington Agency enrollment of the Cheyennes and Arapahos fell to Lieutenant Colonel Thomas Neill and four companies of the 6th Cavalry sent to guard the reservation. By August 1874, the so-called hostiles consisted of approximately 1,800 Cheyennes, 2,000 Comanches, and 1,200 Kiowas. Most of the Arapahos remained peaceful.[24]

From the perspective of the government, at the time, the Red River War can be characterized as one of the most successful wars ever waged by federal troops against the plains tribes. The army pursued the Indians relentlessly during the summer of 1874. A severe drought afflicted the tribesmen as much as it did the troops. With temperatures soaring to 110 degrees, water became scarce and bitterly alkaline. At each point of resistance, cavalry and Indians charged each other. Gatling guns and howitzers raked the Indian lines. By early autumn, storms hit the plains, filling rivers and turning the short-grass prairie into a quagmire. The Cheyennes and their allies long remembered this time as the Wrinkled-Hand Chase.

In September, the relentless Colonel Ranald S. Mackenzie struck against the Indians in Palo Duro Canyon in the Texas Panhandle, a stronghold until then thought to be impregnable. The brilliant attack turned into a rout.

Mackenzie captured supplies along with over 1,400 Indian horses, 1,000 of which he ordered destroyed. Then in November, a detachment under Nelson Miles's command led by First Lieutenant Frank Baldwin surprised Grey Beard's Cheyenne camp of 100 lodges, an action that will be examined in detail in a later chapter. This attack too became a rout, and the troopers destroyed the village. Then in November and December, "northers" swept the Staked Plains. Soldiers and Indians alike suffered terribly from the freezing temperatures.

As early as October, bad weather and military pursuit forced many of the Indians to desert the warring camps and return to the reservations. By January and February the desertions were becoming significant. Some of the Southern Cheyennes, including Medicine Arrows and White Antelope, fled northward to live with the Northern Cheyennes rather than surrender. They began a trend that would occasionally be repeated over the next three years and cause much sensation among white settlers in Kansas, who found themselves in the path of the fleeing southern people. But most of the Cheyennes surrendered to Lieutenant Colonel Neill at the Darlington Agency during February and March. On March 6 alone, 820 Cheyennes surrendered, including Grey Beard, Stone Calf, the old Dog Soldier chief Bull Bear, Minimic, and Medicine Water.[25]

During the course of the Red River War the question arose of what to do with the most flagrant offenders of the peace when they finally surrendered and returned to the reservations. "To turn them loose to renew the same old game in the spring," stated General Sherman, "seems folly."[26] General Sheridan, commander of the Division of the Missouri, favored trial by military commission for all Indians who could be charged with specific acts of murder or theft within the past two years. Other "ringleaders" would be confined away from their people at distant military outposts, where they could not make trouble.

Anticipating the formation of this military commission, officers on the reservations began seizing warriors deemed guilty of murder, theft, or other offenses from each party of Indians who surrendered. At Darlington Agency, the job of arresting individual Cheyennes fell to Lieutenant Colonel Neill, who relied heavily on Indian informers to identify which of their people were guilty of committing offenses.

In April, it became apparent to the Cheyennes what was happening to many of their warriors. It also became apparent that some of those taken into custody were innocent of the charges made against them. Some of the Indians apparently were seized merely to fill quotas. Then, on April 6, 1875, an incident occurred, precipitated by a blacksmith at Darlington Agency, who attempted to place leg irons on a Cheyenne named Black Horse. The indignity Black Horse suffered spurred an escape attempt that in turn ignited a sharp fight between soldiers and many of the Indians on the reservation. The melee that resulted would send some Cheyennes under Little Bull (who did not witness the incident) northward toward Kansas to seek refuge, as Medicine Arrows had done, among their northern brethren.

Notes

1. Stands in Timber and Liberty, *Cheyenne Memories*, 40–41. This story from Cheyenne oral tradition, including a prediction of the coming of horses and domestic cattle (possibly included in the tradition after it originated) remains strong to the present day. Fred Last Bull related this prophecy to Margot Liberty in 1957 almost word for word, as John Stands in Timber remembered the story.

2. Quoted in Nye, *Carbine & Lance*, 157. For a concise overview of the influence the Quakers had on the Grant peace policy and how that policy affected the Red River War, see Utley, *Frontier Regulars*, 207–210. See also Robert M. Utley, *The Indian Frontier of the American West, 1846–1890* (Albuquerque: University of New Mexico Press, 1984), 129–155.

3. Utley, *Frontier Regulars*, 209.

4. House, *Annual Report of the Commissioner of Indian Affairs for the Year 1874*, 43rd Cong., 1st sess., 1874, H. Doc. 1, serial 1639, 233.

5. Ibid., 234.

6. Hyde, *Life of George Bent*, 355.

7. James L. Haley, *The Buffalo War: The History of the Red River Indian Uprising of 1874* (New York: Doubleday, 1976), 46.

8. All the events leading to Cheyenne participation in the Red River War are synthesized in Powell, *People of the Sacred Mountain*, 2:846–860.

9. Haley, *The Buffalo War*, 27.

10. Powell, *People of the Sacred Mountain*, 2:851.

11. Berthrong, *The Southern Cheyennes*, 381.

12. Powell, *People of the Sacred Mountain*, 2:852.

13. Haley, *The BuffaloWar*, 26–27.

14. Ibid., 27.

15. Ibid., 34–36.

16. Powell, *People of the Sacred Mountain*, 2:853.

17. Quoted in Powell, *People of the Sacred Mountain*, 2:854.

18. The Battle of Adobe Walls and the entire Red River War is well chronicled. It is beyond the scope of the present study to rehash it in minute detail. It is briefly surveyed here as a precursor to the flight of the Cheyennes north to Sappa Creek early in 1875 and of the resultant, less well chronicled, events that culminated in the fight on Sappa Creek in April 1875.

Sources for the treatment of Adobe Walls include Grinnell, *The Fighting Cheyennes*, 323–324; Hyde, *Life of George Bent*, 357–360; and the accounts of Comanche informants Timbo, Yellow Fish, and Poafebitty, in Nye, *Carbine & Lance*, 245. Original sources for white accounts of the battle include Olive K. Dixon, *Life of "Billy" Dixon, Plainsman, Scout, and Pioneer* (Dallas: P. L. Turner Co., 1914), 155–187. See also Haley, *The BuffaloWar*, 65–78 and Powell, *People of the Sacred Mountain*, 2:852–860.

19. Dixon, *Life of "Billy" Dixon*, 167–168.

20. Grinnell, *The Fighting Cheyennes*, 324; quoted in Powell, *People of the Sacred Mountain*, 2:859.

21. Grinnell, *The Fighting Cheyennes*, 324; Hyde, *Life of George Bent*, 360. Sources vary. In *The Buffalo War*, Haley claims seventy Indian casualties. A scout with the Baldwin Expedition reported seeing thirty Indian graves around Adobe Walls. Exact figures will never be known. For an overview of the incident, see Powell, *People of the Sacred Mountain*, 2:1350 n. 75.

22. Quoted in Powell, *People of the Sacred Mountain*, 2:1350 n. 79. See also General Nelson A. Miles, *Personal Recollections & Observations of General Nelson A. Miles* (Lincoln: University of Nebraska Press, 1992), I:163.

23. Utley, *Frontier Regulars*, 214.

24. Ibid., 220–221.

25. There are a few excellent studies of the Red River War prior to Sappa Creek. One of the best is Haley, *The BuffaloWar*. An excellent brief synthesis is found in Utley, *Frontier Regulars*, 219–235.

26. Quoted in Utley, *Frontier Regulars*, 229.

———

Chapter III

The Promised Land

I could not cry. There wasn't tears enough in my eyes.

—Julia German, age seven, remembering the death of her
parents and her capture by Medicine Water, September 11, 1874

In late summer 1874, two events took place in western Kansas that ultimately concluded with the mismanagement at Darlington Agency the following April that sent Little Bull and other Cheyennes fleeing north, where they met destruction on the banks of Sappa Creek. During the summer campaigns in the south, at least two bands of Cheyenne warriors broke through Colonel Miles's lines of envelopment on the Staked Plains and moved into Kansas to strike the whites they blamed for the Red River War. But instead of soldiers, horse thieves, and buffalo hunters, the Indians found only unsuspecting settlers.

They struck dramatically in southwestern Kansas, near the border with Indian Territory, in what came to be called the Lone Tree Massacre. Later, the same band committed the German Massacre near Fort Wallace, the most publicized Indian attack on white civilians in Kansas history. This group was led by Medicine Water, head of the Bowstring society. With him were sixteen men and his wife, *Mochi*, "Buffalo Calf Woman," a woman warrior who had survived the Sand Creek Massacre but had lost most of her family there, including her first husband. Another young woman was in the raiding party, the niece of Stone Calf. She was in the company of her husband. Among the men were Yellow Horse, son of Chief Sand Hill; White Man; Rising Bull; Lone Tree; Bear's Heart; Lame Man (*Cohoe*—Broken Leg, or Limpy); Little Shield; Chief Killer, who was Medicine Water's son-in-law; Big Moccasin; Squint Eyes; and Kicking Horse, a Northern Cheyenne.[1]

The luckless whites who first suffered the wrath of Medicine Water's band consisted of part of a work crew contracted by the government to finish a geographical survey of southwestern Kansas. Oliver Short and his fourteen-year-old son, Daniel, set out from Fort Dodge on August 24. With them were Harry Jones, John Keuchler, James Shaw, and Shaw's eighteen-year-old son, Allen. Two days later, on August 26, friends found their bodies on the open plains. Apparently the surveyors had tried to make a run for safety, because there were twenty-eight bullet holes in their wagon and the oxen were found dead at their yokes with their hindquarters cut off. Short's son and Jones were scalped, as was Oliver Short, whose head was smashed in with his own survey compass. The bodies were buried on the plains in Meade County near a single cottonwood tree that for many years into the twentieth century marked the location of the "Lone Tree Massacre." Eventually Short's widow won a $10,000 claim she had filed against the State of Kansas for her loss.[2]

Medicine Water's band struck next on the old Smoky Hill wagon road not far from Fort Wallace, in country that had seen so much fighting between the 7th Cavalry and the Dog Soldiers in 1867. The family of John German (sometimes spelled Germaine in early reports) was originally from Georgia but had spent the past year slowly making their way from Elgin to Russell, Kansas. Now they were en route to new opportunities in Colorado Territory. On September 11, 1874, the family was about a day east of Fort Wallace, six miles from the modern town of Russell Springs in Logan County, when Medicine Water's Cheyennes descended on their single wagon in the early morning light. There were nine in the German family: John; his wife, Lydia; one son, Stephen, nineteen; and daughters Rebecca Jane, twenty; Catherine, seventeen; Joanna, fifteen; Sophia, twelve; Julia, seven; and Adelaide, called Addie by her sisters, five.[3]

The bloodletting was over in a few moments. John German was shot first. Lydia was killed by a tomahawk while trying to run away. Stephen, one of the first to die, was shot while trying to escape to a nearby ravine. Both parents were scalped while they were still alive. Then Medicine Water's wife, Buffalo Calf Woman, sank an ax into John German's head and left it there. Meanwhile, twenty-year-old Rebecca attacked one of the warriors with an ax but was knocked unconscious. She was gang raped and killed before the Indians departed. Joanna was shot and scalped. The warriors plundered and burned the wagon, drove off the cattle, and rode away with Catherine, Sophie, Julia, and Addie as prisoners.[4]

The war party moved south, back toward the panhandle of Indian Territory. Late that afternoon the Indians divided the captives. Stone Calf's niece and her husband took Julia and Addie to raise as their own children. One of the young warriors, whose name is not known, claimed Sophia, and seventeen-year-old Catherine was claimed by Medicine Water. "Then they bridled up the horses," Julia told a reporter three months later, "and put sister [Addie] in front of one young buck and me in front [of] another on horseback. We were jolted until our necks got stiff."[5]

That night Medicine Water and his companion raped Catherine and Sophia German. Nor were these two older sisters treated well when the war party reached a larger camp after they had crossed south out of Kansas. On one occasion Catherine was stripped, painted, and tied onto a horse by one of the Cheyenne women in the camp. Then she was "put on the prairie," as the Cheyenne called this accepted cultural practice. Several young men in the camp rode her down and raped her. Catherine German later said that during her captivity she was violated by "nearly all in the tribe."[6]

A few days after the massacre Medicine Water's band joined the other war party that had entered Kansas and attacked a group of cattlemen on the Arkansas River near Larkin, Kansas. Soon troops from Fort Dodge pushed the Cheyennes south and eventually toward the North Canadian River in the Texas Panhandle. There, to expedite the flight southward, the Cheyennes abandoned on the plains the two younger German girls, Addie and Julia.[7]

"We lived for six weeks with what we could find on the prairie and along the streams," Addie remembered years later. "Wild grapes, hackberries, wild plums, wild onions, even grass was pulled up and the tender lower ends eaten . . ."[8] Eventually the girls discovered a recent military campsite, where they found some "scattered grains and scraps of food." In October, three Cheyenne wolves found the starving girls and took them to the village of Grey Beard on McClellan Creek near present-day Pampa, Texas.[9] When Addie and Julia reached Grey Beard's village, they were reunited with their sister Sophia. When Medicine Water's band reached Grey Beard's village, the band divided. The warrior who had claimed Sophia remained with Grey Beard and later traded Sophia to Wolf Robe, who took her as a wife.[10]

Meanwhile, Medicine Water and most of the Bowstring society crossed the Staked Plains and joined the village of the peace chief Stone Calf. With Medicine Water was Long Black, a prominent warrior who had taken a liking to Catherine and claimed her from Medicine Water.[11]

During the autumn of 1874, the camps of the People moved often to avoid Colonel Nelson A. Miles's ever-tightening noose. In October, Miles divided his troops into three columns that swept eastward across the Texas Panhandle in an attempt to drive the Cheyennes and their allies into converging troops operating along the border of Texas and Indian Territory.

In November, a column led by First Lieutenant Frank D. Baldwin found Grey Beard's Suhtai village on McClellan Creek. Baldwin's command comprised D Company, 6th Cavalry, and D Company, 5th Infantry, which was being transported in converted supply wagons along with a few scouts. Baldwin's prompt action probably saved the lives of Addie and Julia German.

Strategically positioning the infantry at an oblique angle slightly behind and on the flank of the cavalry, Baldwin ordered a charge. The Cheyennes deployed a skirmish line in front of the village, buying time for women and children to evacuate along with the pony herd. The Indian skirmishers fell back slowly on the village and then fled to the brow of a hill behind the camp, where they rallied and tried to retake the village with a concentrated counterattack. But a second massed cavalry charge routed them.

Baldwin pursued the Cheyennes and broke off the attack only after a four-hour running fight. Baldwin's command suffered no casualties. Only

one Cheyenne casualty is known. Years later, Addie German vividly recalled the circumstances of that warrior's death. Returning to the village,
the soldiers found Addie and Julia German. The Cheyenne women had
taken Sophia during the onset of the attack.[12] During the running battle,
a lone warrior returned to the abandoned village. Upon seeing the approach of the Indian, Julia hid under a buffalo robe. The warrior "shot at
where Julia lay, sick and exhausted," Addie remembered. "A soldier shot
the Indian then went to see what he had shot at and found her." Addie
heard the shot while "hunting something to keep up a fire," and came
running to see if her sister was still alive, "though I fell down quite often,"
she admitted, in her anxious dash to reach her sister.[13]

The hearts of the soldiers went out to the little girls, for they were
weak and emaciated. One teamster with the command remarked as tears
rolled down his cheeks: "I have driven my mules over these plains for
three months, but I will stay forever or until we get them other girls."[14]
The soldiers took the girls to Camp Supply, Indian Territory, and later the
army escorted them to Fort Leavenworth, Kansas. For his prompt and decisive action, First Lieutenant Baldwin, who possessed one Medal of Honor
for his Civil War service, won a second for saving Addie and Julia German
from Grey Beard's village on November 8, 1874.[15]

The rescue of Addie and Julia was the first solid evidence the military
attained that any of the German daughters had survived. Earlier in September, two residents of Ellsworth, Kansas, had discovered the site of the German Massacre and reported it to authorities at Fort Wallace. Immediately a
party under Second Lieutenant C. C. Hewitt left the fort to recover the bodies. Hewitt found a family Bible that was later returned to the surviving
German sisters. Hewitt ascertained from the genealogy in the Bible that the
family numbered nine. He had found only five bodies, "badly devoured by
wolves."[16] The remains were interred at Fort Wallace where, in 1959, the
maintained grave was marked with a large marble headstone.

The bitter winter of 1874–1875, along with Colonel Nelson Miles's
relentless pursuit, brought much suffering to the warring plains tribes. Bands
surrendered continuously through the winter and early spring. In January
three Cheyennes came in to Darlington Agency and reported that Chief Stone

Calf wished to surrender. They told Agent John Miles that Sophia German was with Grey Beard's Suhtai, and Catherine was in Stone Calf's village. Lieutenant Colonel Thomas H. Neill dispatched Indian runners to all the Cheyenne camps, informing them that Addie and Julia had been recovered and that Stone Calf and his followers would be received favorably at the agency only if Sophia and Catherine were alive and unharmed. Neill's verbal message included instructions to the older girls to read his written message to Stone Calf and Grey Beard.[17]

Colonel Miles also sent a message into the villages with a Kiowa runner instructing Grey Beard that Miles would hold him personally accountable for any harm to Catherine and Sophia. Catherine later recalled that "Chief Stone Calf received the message and informed Chief Gray [sic] Beard who in turn commanded his followers that special watchful care must be taken of Sophia."[18] Stone Calf promised Catherine the same treatment. Colonel Miles also sent a personal message to Catherine and Sophia on January 20. "Your little sisters are well and in the hands of friends," he told them. "Do not be discouraged. Every effort is being made for your welfare."[19]

By midwinter 1875 the plight of the German girls was making national headlines. On March 6, Stone Calf, Grey Beard, and the main body of Southern Cheyennes, some 1,600 in number, including those who had committed the German Massacre, surrendered to Lieutenant Colonel Neill at Darlington Agency. Army ambulances conveyed Catherine and Sophia German to the safety of the Darlington Agency hospital.

"The surrender was a beautiful sight," Neill wrote in his official report. "Stone Calf in front with a white flag was followed by a line of three divisions of Indians on foot . . . they halted, threw down their arms in line on the ground and then sat down . . ."[20] But the Quaker Indian agent at Darlington, John D. Miles, although recognizing with classic Victorian logic the inevitability of their plight, saw Stone Calf's people differently. "A more wretched and poverty-stricken community than these it would be difficult to imagine," he remembered. "Bereft of lodges, and the most ordinary of cooking apparatus; with no ponies . . . half starved . . . scarcely anything that could be called clothing, they were truly objects of pity . . . for the first time the Cheyennes seemed to realize the power of the Government, and their own inability to cope successfully therewith."[21]

After recovering for three months at Darlington, Catherine and Sophia joined Addie and Julia at Fort Leavenworth. By then Catherine had turned eighteen. The girls' grandfather in Georgia, Thomas German, requested custody of the three younger sisters, but they preferred to remain with Catherine in Kansas. For a time Colonel Miles held court-appointed custody as official guardian of Addie, Sophia, and Julia. But upon his transfer to the northern plains in 1876 during the Great Sioux War, he relinquished guardianship to Mr. and Mrs. Patrick Corney of Leavenworth, Kansas. Almost immediately the federal government appropriated $10,000 from the budget slated for the Southern Cheyennes at Darlington Agency to be used for the girls' compensation.[22]

All four sisters eventually married, raised families, and lived long lives. Catherine and Julia resided in California. Sophia moved to Nebraska, and Addie remained in Kansas. Over the years their descendants wrote of the sisters' experiences with the Cheyennes.[23]

The Lone Tree and German Massacres, and especially the ordeal and captivity of the four German sisters became a cause célèbre that crystallized public opinion against the Indians in the Red River War. Those events caused the Southern Cheyennes far more trouble in the long run than they bargained for. Army troops that previously had been well disposed or ambivalent toward the cause of the plains tribes with respect to the destruction of the buffalo now relentlessly pursued the Southern Cheyennes in order to liberate the German sisters. Many Indians, including the blameless, would suffer repercussions because of the German ordeal and the nationwide publicity it generated: imprisonment in Florida, and for some, flight to the north and death along the valley of Sappa Creek.[24]

The Germans were indeed unfortunate victims—in the wrong place during a unique, and amazingly short, point in time. If the Germans had been in the western quarter of Kansas just six years earlier they would have traveled through an incredibly rich zone of cultural interaction, a land teeming with buffalo, a place cherished by both the northern and southern plains tribes. From Fort Wallace to the forks of the Republican River to the north, Cheyennes, both the northern and southern people, gathered to hunt and renew friendships with the Arapahos and Brulé Sioux. In that game-abundant valley these peoples gathered to camp under a seemingly endless panorama of sky and plains. The Republican Valley, especially, had served as an age-old neutral or transition zone for the Cheyennes and their Lakota allies. The valley was a favorite hunting ground of the Dog Soldier military society, once the most formidable armed force ever assembled by the Cheyenne people. From Waconda Springs in Kansas to the Colorado high plains along the South Platte, the Dog Soldiers had defended this land against the whites at such engagements as Julesburg, Prairie Dog Creek, Beecher Island, and Beaver Creek, only to meet destruction in July 1869 at Summit Springs.[25]

The years 1867 and 1868 were the bloodiest in the history of western Kansas, as the Dog Soldiers swept out of the Republican Valley and descended upon the settlements in the Solomon and Saline valleys, only to take refuge again amid the vastness of the Republican River country. A shortage of army troops in the West during the height of Reconstruction in the defeated Confederate states meant that undermanned elements of the recently formed 7th and 10th Cavalry regiments (in 1866) or Kansas volunteer regiments could rarely catch up to the Dog Soldiers.[26] Had the Germans been traveling the Smoky Hill Road during these years they would have found the Indian war parties much larger, their own fate much more commonplace, and the headlines of the penny press not quite so sensationally focused on them.

As it was in 1874, however, the German Massacre was viewed by the press as an anachronism, an act of barbarism from a bygone era that was positively antique. One Kansas newspaper carried Julia's story under the headline, "A Little Girl's Tale of Suffering and Horror."[27] Since the Dog Soldiers' decimation in 1869 relative peace had come to northwest Kansas. Across their former hunting domain now stretched three railroads, the Union Pacific along the Platte corridor to the north, William Jackson Palmer's Kansas Pacific in the central corridor along the Smoky Hill route, and on the south, along the Arkansas River, the Atchison, Topeka and Santa Fe. The Santa Fe Railroad capitalized on the buffalo slaughter of the previous two years, rendering the once rich lands comparatively barren for roving bands of Indian hunters.* More troops were in the West in 1874. The presence of the railroads meant that the resources of a mighty expansionist nation and the manpower of at least two military departments could be mobilized from all directions within a few hours to ovrepower any Indian raiders venturing into western Kansas.

Perhaps in no other place on the Great Plains was the physical integrity of the natural habitat more drastically altered in such a short time by buffalo slaughter, military conquest, and settled agriculture as in western Kansas during the late 1860s and the 1870s. The changes just as drastically altered the habits and mobility patterns of the Native American peoples who survived what constituted an ecological catastrophe and genocide. The census of 1870 revealed a population increase of 239.9 percent in Kansas over the previous decade. More than a small portion of this increase occurred in the western portion of the state.[28] By the early 1870s the population density of Kansas rose from 1.3 persons per square mile in 1860 to 4.5 persons per square mile.[29] Although the great Solomon Valley raids of 1868 had occurred along the line of newly organized counties abutting the one-hundredth meridian, roughly the western one-quarter of remaining unorganized lands in Kansas to the west of that "frontier line" still afforded prime buffalo range and campsites for the Indians. As long as the buffalo still roamed there was little incentive for warrior societies like the Dog Soldiers to settle on the reservation lands in Indian Territory that were agreed upon at the 1867 Treaty of Medicine Lodge.

But with the destruction of both the Dog Soldiers and their primary cultural resource, the buffalo, the remaining lands in western Kansas were quickly organized. Eighteen new counties west of the one-hundredth meridian appeared on the map of Kansas in 1873 alone.[30] The tide of western expansion would have quickly engulfed those remaining lands, but there was a lull in growth in 1873 and 1874 during which the perceived destiny of white farmers appeared, however briefly, not quite so manifest.

---

* The Union Pacific and Santa Fe Railroads marked the rough borders of the Southern Cheyenne homelands between the Arkansas and the Platte, with the Kansas Pacific Railroad bisecting them.

Three factors stalled even moderate settlement into new counties in the western quarter of Kansas during the early 1870s—drought, depression, and grasshoppers. Since the expansion of the 1860s and 1870s was essentially to free land, the Panic of 1873 had less effect on western Kansas than later depressions, when more landholdings were mortgaged. But drought and grasshoppers were different matters.[31] The searing drought of 1874 was the precursor to the great plague of millions of Rocky Mountain locusts that swept the plains states that summer. Eventually the insects cut a swath of destruction 250 miles wide, moving from Texas to the Dakotas and devastating over 5,000 square miles of cropland. Kansas in 1874 became a wasteland, and starvation was a real possibility for more than a few of the state's farmers.[32]

At times the locust swarms blackened the sun. Settlers reported seeing what they thought were storm fronts moving across the sky only to have the "storm front" descend on their fields and destroy everything within a day. Marsh Murdock of Wichita watched the insects in "untold millions, in clouds upon clouds, until their fluttering wings looked like a sweeping snow storm in the heavens, . . . until their dark bodies covered everything green upon the earth."[33] With such troubled times in the "promised land," settlement on the high plains slowed to a trickle west of the ravished croplands; what few whites were there had little time to contemplate the moral vicissitudes of the Red River War to the south. Those who ventured west, like the German family, headed toward Colorado Territory.

It is possible that the Germans, or for that matter most of the settlers who came to Kansas after 1870, had never seen an Indian. Thinking the "Buffalo War" was concentrated in the panhandles across the southern border, the Germans pushed west naively and found themselves alone, without any hope of assistance. The nightmares of childhood captivity myths were surely awakened in their minds at the first sight of Medicine Water's war party, a condition that must have made their encounter only more horrible.

The series of events that combined to create the demographic inertia on the high plains in 1874 came to benefit the Cheyennes between 1874 and 1875 to a degree that would embarrass the federal government and renew the fears of settlers in Kansas who had thought their problems with the Indians were a thing of the past. By separating the southern people on the Darlington

Agency in Indian Territory from their northern brethren who attached themselves to one of the Lakota agencies in the north, the government bought itself considerable trouble. For between the agencies in the south and those in the north were the sparsely settled lands of extreme western Kansas that were devoid of reservations and Indians and awaiting a renewal of white expansion that indeed resumed after 1875.

Essentially, the government unwittingly set up a relatively unpopulated escape route along this high plains corridor for Southern Cheyennes fleeing the Red River War, evading pursuing troops, or seeking revenge on isolated prey, a practice that repeated itself more than once between 1874 and 1875. This situation was potentially explosive in that war parties bent on vengeance, like that of Medicine Water's, if left unchecked could easily turn on the lines of sparse white settlement in western Kansas. For more peaceful bands, the same corridor would serve as a route of travel for both northern and southern people living on the reservations, so-called stampeders going back and forth to visit families and friends as they had done for decades. Misunderstandings resulting from the encroachment of white settlement into the corridor could prove dangerous for the Indians. But amid the intense hardship, warfare, and stress that existed in 1874, non-Indians who found themselves crossing paths with a party of warring Cheyennes—who remembered what the land looked like before the white hide hunters, when it teemed with buffalo, when the Dog Soldiers called it their own—were likely to forfeit their lives as the Indians took revenge for the enormity of the ecological and social upheaval.

So it was that as Stone Calf and Grey Beard surrendered at the conclusion of the winter of 1874–1875, some freedom-loving Cheyennes not yet completely resigned to subjugation and acculturation looked to the unsettled lands of the Dog Soldiers in western Kansas and considered that well-known ground a route to safety among the Lakotas and their own relatives and friends in the north.

THE SAND HILL FIGHT

Lieutenant Colonel Neill sent the bands of Stone Calf and Grey Beard to camp along the North Fork of the Canadian River about three miles above Darlington Agency. With the Cheyennes were remnants of the once mighty Dog Soldiers under their head, White Horse, a renowned warrior who had fought the whites since the 1860s and had lost several members of his family in the Beecher Island fight in Colorado's Republican Valley in 1868. Neill placed a guard on the Indians to keep them separate from the peaceful bands on the reservation under Old Whirlwind and Little Robe. The soldiers, under the command of Captain Andrew Bennett, 5th Infantry, lived in dugouts next to Stone Calf's and Grey Beard's camps throughout the winter of 1875 and issued rations to the People as prisoners of war.[34]

Not long after Stone Calf's surrender, divisional military authorities acting under instructions from the president of the United States ordered that "the ringleaders [of the Red River War] and such as have been guilty of crimes" would be "selected and sent to such military posts as may hereafter be designated. They are not to be accompanied by their families."[35] In selecting the "guilty" Indians, priority would be given to finding those individuals who allegedly committed depredations on civilians in Kansas and elsewhere during the previous year. As it turned out, the last statement in the order proved crucial.

The army chose Fort Marion, Florida, for the incarceration of the Indians. Although the process of identifying alleged guilty parties among the Kiowas and Comanches at Fort Sill, in Indian Territory, went smoothly, such was not the case with the Southern Cheyennes at Darlington. Colonel Nelson A. Miles, who was supposed to oversee the selection, was on leave, and the task fell to Lieutenant Colonel Neill.

One morning in early April, Neill's soldiers rounded up all the men in Stone Calf's village. With Neill were the two elder German sisters, Catherine and Sophia. They studied the faces of the Indians carefully. Now they would have their justice. Lieutenant Colonel Neill, too, relished this emotional time of revenge. "I took the two German Girls, Catherine and Sophia," Neill reported, "and made them examine carefully and thoroughly the face of every man of the tribe to discover and identify the murderers of their father, mother, brother and two sisters and those who had injured and maltreated [them]."[36] But the sisters recognized only a few Cheyennes as having participated in

the massacre of their parents or treated them cruelly during their captivity.
They were Medicine Water; his wife, Buffalo Calf Woman, who had split
John German's head open with an ax; Long Black, who had held and
abused the German girls in the later months of their captivity; White Man,
who had participated directly in the killings at Lone Tree; Rising Bull; Big
Moccasin; Lame Man (*Cohoe*); Chief Killer; and Bears Heart, who was be-
trayed by Big Moccasin and Medicine Water when it looked as if he might
escape recognition. Medicine Water suggested to Neill that some of the
participants in the German Massacre might have already escaped to the
north.[37]

After the German sisters had finished their identifications, however, the
selection process became a sham. Eventually thirty-three Cheyennes were
selected, mostly through hearsay from Indian informants or by unsubstantiated accusations by whites, or simply because they were chiefs and therefore deemed to be ringleaders. In that way Grey Beard was selected, as was
Minimic and Heap of Birds.[38] The increasingly indiscriminate process went
on until nightfall and "horrified" acting agent J. A. Covington, standing in
for Agent John D. Miles who was on official leave. "Considerable time was
consumed," Covington wrote in his report, and "night came on before the
list was completed and Genl. Neil [sic], in order to get his complement of
prisoners . . . ordered eighteen struck off from the right" of the line to fill
the quota. This process, Covington protested, was made "irrespective of name,
rank, or character . . . That a number of apparently innocent parties were
selected, there can be no doubt."[39] By Neill's side serving as an interpreter
was the Hispanic scout Raphael Romero (nicknamed Romeo), who later
confessed to George Bent that Lieutenant Colonel Neill was "under the influence of liquor at the time, and this the Indians [genuinely] believe."[40]

On the morning of April 6, 1875, the prisoners were led out of the
guardhouse to be shackled in preparation for their journey by prison train
to Fort Marion, Florida.[41] The Cheyenne prisoners were escorted to the
Darlington Agency blacksmith by a guard detail of the 5th Infantry under
Captain Andrew Bennett. The blacksmith was an African American named
Wesley, who proceeded to place manacles on the ankles of each Cheyenne.
Soon troubled erupted. Sitting nearby, watching Wesley shackle the men,

several Cheyenne women began chanting war songs urging the men to break free and to fight and die like brave warriors of the People. Never, before the coming of the whites to the plains, had the Cheyennes or their enemies embraced the Euro-American concept of criminal arrest and incarceration. An enemy allowed his male adversary the dignity of dying as a warrior on the field of battle—only women and children were made prisoners. For the Cheyenne men and chiefs who found themselves shackled in iron that day, the experience was emasculating. The ultimate humiliation came when their own women began chanting, thus insinuating their cowardice.[42]

A few of the men had already been placed in irons when a high-spirited young warrior named Black Horse could stand the taunts from the women no more. As Wesley was about to place a leg iron on his ankle, Black Horse kicked the blacksmith under the chin and jumped onto a nearby horse to make his escape. Black Horse headed toward White Horse's nearby camp. The guards opened fire. Bullets ripped into the tepees in White Horse's camp, and his Dog Soldiers ran around frantically, not knowing what was happening. Before he could reach the Dog Soldiers a bullet struck Black Horse, and he fell, wounded in the side.[43]

White Horse's village was on the north bank of the North Fork of the Canadian River. When the fighting began, the guard of the 5th Infantry was reinforced by M Company, 6th Cavalry under Captain William A. Rafferty, and two companies of Buffalo Soldiers, Companies M and D, 10th Cavalry, under Captains S. T. Norvell and A. S. Keyes, respectively.[44] Immediately, the remnants of the Dog Soldiers in White Horse's village, along with their women, began digging rifle pits. They uncovered a few hidden weapons, and the Dog Soldiers prepared to defend their village as they had tried to do so valiantly in 1869 at Summit Springs. As more bullets ripped into the camp, however, the Indians prepared to evacuate. About 150 to 200 men and women crossed the river to the south side and began to entrench in a sand hill near the river while other Dog Soldiers covered their line of retreat. The warrior Big Shell did not escape, George Bent (who was in the village) remembered. As Big Shell came out of his lodge, confused over the source of the first rifle volleys, Bent rode up to him just as a 5th Infantryman hit Big Shell in the head with a well-placed bullet.[45]

About 2:00 P.M., Captain Rafferty ordered his 6th Cavalry to dismount and approach the village on foot, thinking the Dog Soldiers had few weapons and could not long keep up the fight. A furious volley from the Indians convinced him otherwise. The two companies of Buffalo Soldiers came up on the southwest of the camp, and, with Rafferty on the east, the soldiers attempted to flank the village. A steady volley from the troopers into the Cheyenne camp did not deter the Dog Soldiers, who repulsed the attack on their position. About 2:30, Lieutenant Colonel Neill reached the fight and ordered Second Lieutenant Frank S. Hinkle, 5th Infantry, to bring up a Gatling gun and rake the village.

Again the 6th Cavalry troopers moved on the village, but the Buffalo Soldiers were not in a good position to support them. The revolving-barrel Gatling gun raked the Dog Soldiers for a second time from 400 yards. Then Neill ordered a massed charge. Once again, the Dog Soldiers beat the troops off. With dusk approaching, Neill's command withdrew. The soldiers sustained nineteen wounded, six seriously. Private Clark Young, a Buffalo Soldier in M Company, 10th Cavalry died later of his wounds. Neill later reported five Cheyenne men and one woman dead.[46] The Indians claimed only two dead, Little Bear and Dirty Nose. An unknown number, including Black Horse and Big Shell, were wounded.[47]

During the night of April 6, Neill brought up what reinforcements he could muster from Darlington Agency, but under the cover of a heavy thunderstorm the people in the Cheyenne breastworks sneaked through the lines to safety in the villages of Whirlwind and Little Robe, close to the agency. The next morning when Neill's troops approached the sand hill they found the rifle pits deserted. For a final time the Dog Soldiers had successfully defended the Southern Cheyennes.[48]

Not all the Indians who escaped from the sand hill defenses that night found their way into the villages of the agency peace chiefs. A few decided to flee north through the Kansas escape corridor to a life with their northern kin. Early the next morning these people found a camp of Cheyennes under Little Bull, a Suhtai who had been a member of Grey Beard's band.

Little Bull had not surrendered with Grey Beard that winter but instead had decided to make a dash through the army lines into Kansas and the Northern Cheyenne villages in the north. Little Bull, described by George Bent as a great warrior, was camped on the North Fork of the Canadian River about twenty-five miles from the agency when the panic stricken refugees from White Horse's village stumbled into his camp.[49]

Due to the fighting in the sand hill and the panicked flight of White Horse's followers, Little Bull decided to leave for the north at once. How many of White Horse's people stayed with Little Bull and how many went back to Darlington Agency is unknown. But the remarkable chain of events beginning with the Lone Tree and German massacres in Kansas the previous year in part led to the government's decision to punish and humiliate the "ringleaders" of the Red River War by incarcerating them far from their homeland. The ineptitude of Lieutenant Colonel Neill in executing his orders arguably made the escape north inevitable. Neill's actions launched several groups of Southern Cheyennes northward along the western periphery of the Kansas settlements in an attempt to reach the northern agencies. Some were successful. Some returned. The migration of both northern and southern people back and forth along the western Kansas corridor was noticeable in 1875. For Little Bull's band, however, tragedy awaited.

Notes

1. John Sipes (Oklahoma State Historical Society) to Arlene Feldmann Jauken, undated list of Cheyenne participants in the German Massacre, photocopy in the Wray Museum, Wray, Colorado (hereafter referred to as "Sipes's List"). Jauken, a descendent of the German sisters, requested the information from Sipes while researching her ancestors. For another account by a relative who knew the Germans personally, although it contains some errors, see Grace E. Meredith, ed., *Girl Captives of the Cheyennes: A True Story of the Capture and Rescue of Four Frontier Girls* (Los Angeles: Gem Publishing Co., 1927), 17ff. See also for the names of participants in the German Massacre Powell, *People of the Sacred Mountain*, 2:867–868. Powell's names and Sipes's names are almost identical.

2. Mrs. F. C. Montgomery, "United States Surveyors Massacred by Indians," *Kansas Historical Quarterly* 1 (1931): 266–272; Haley, *The Buffalo War*, 142.

3. *Leavenworth Daily Times*, December 3, 1874; Adelaide German to Helen Meyer, Bern, Kansas, March 10, 1930, Kansas State Historical Society (hereafter referred to as "Addie's Account").

4. Meredith, *Girl Captives of the Cheyennes*, 17–31; Powell, *People of the Sacred Mountain*, 2:868–869; Lonnie J. White, "White Women Captives of the Southern Plains Indians, 1866–1875," *Journal of the West* 8, no. 3 (July 1969): 346–347.

5. *Leavenworth Daily Times*, December 3, 1874.

6. Meredith, *Girl Captives of the Cheyennes*, 20–21. Cheyenne historian Peter John Powell states that "this mistreating of captive women was not unusual among the People. Their women were famous for their chastity and the men respected it. However, white women were a different matter They had come to join their men in seizing the People's land and buffalo. So the two oldest girls were treated in the way [Cheyenne] women of bad repute were treated." Powell, *People of the Sacred Mountain*, 2.869. The Cheyenne custom of "putting on the prairie" (gang raping) unchaste women of the tribe is explained by Hoebel, *The Cheyennes*, 95–96.

7. *Kansan*, September 17, 1874.

8. Addie's Account.

9. Ibid.; White, "White Women Captives," 347.

10. Meredith, *Girl Captives of the Cheyennes*, 33.

11. *Topeka Capitol*, May 2, 1937; Powell, *People of the Sacred Mountain*, 2:870–871.

12. First Lieutenant Frank D. Baldwin, diary entry November 8–9, 1874, copy in the Wray Museum, Wray, Colorado.

13. Addie's Account.

14. Miles, *Personal Recollections*, 175.

15. W. F. Beyer and O. F. Keydel, *Deeds of Valor*, vol. 1 (Detroit: The Perrien Keydel Co.), 179–184.

16. NARA, U.S. Army Continental Commands, RG 94, Second Lieutenant C. C. Hewitt to Post Adjutant, Fort Wallace, October 2, 1874, copy in the Wray Museum, Wray, Colorado. For Fort Wallace see Mrs. F. C. Montgomery, "Fort Wallace and Its Relation to the Frontier," *Kansas Historical Collections* 17 (1926–1928): 189–283.

17. White, "White Women Captives," 349.

18. Meredith, *Girl Captives of the Cheyennes*, 105.

19. Miles, *Personal Recollections*, 176.

20. NARA, Adjutant General's Office, RG 94, File 3490, Neill to the assistant adjutant general, Department of the Missouri, March 7, 1875.

21. House, *Annual Report of the Commissioner of Indian Affairs for the Year 1875*, 43rd Cong., 2nd sess., 1875, H. Doc. 1, serial 1680, 269.

22. Ibid., 268–269.

23. Meredith, *Girl Captives of the Cheyennes*, 110–114.

24. Hyde, *Life of George Bent*, 363.

25. For a discussion of the Republican Valley as a cultural transition zone and a complete overview of the warfare between Dog Soldiers and whites in the late 1860s, see John H. Monnett, *The Battle of Beecher Island*.

26. Ibid., 57–58.

27. *Leavenworth Daily Times*, December 3, 1874.

28. William F. Zornow, *Kansas: A History of the Jayhawk State* (Norman: University of Oklahoma Press, 1957), 162.

29. Ibid., 163.

30. Homer E. Socolofsky and Huber Self, *Historical Atlas of Kansas*, 2nd ed. (Norman: University of Oklahoma Press, 1988), 40–41. For county dates of origin, see Sondra Van Meter McCoy and Jan Hults, *1001 Kansas Place Names* (Lawrence: University Press of Kansas, 1989).

31. Zornow, *Kansas: A History*, 163.

32. See Craig Miner, *West of Wichita: Settling the High Plains of Kansas, 1865–1890* (Lawrence: University Press of Kansas, 1986), 53. This is by far the best single history of western Kansas.

33. *Wichita Eagle*, August 13, 1874. Quoted in Miner, *West of Wichita*, 52.

34. Grinnell, *The Fighting Cheyennes*, 325.

35. W. W. Belknap, secretary of war, memorandum for a telegram to General W. T. Sherman, located by Powell, *People of the Sacred Mountain*, 2:897.

36. NARA, Adjutant General's Office, RG 94, Neill to Colonel R. Williams, assistant adjutant general, Department of the Missouri, March 13, 1875. (Copy on file in the Wray Museum, Wray, Colorado.)

37. Sipes's List. Sipes specifically identifies these people as members of Medicine Water's band who were sent to the federal prison at Fort Marion, Florida.

38. Hyde, *Life of George Bent*, 364–365.

39. Covington's memorandum is quoted in Haley, *The Buffalo War*, 215.

40. Hyde, *Life of George Bent*, 365.

41. Hyde, *Life of George Bent*, 365. Haley claims in *The Buffalo War*, 215, that the prisoners were shackled on the same day they were arrested. In any event, the Sand Hill fight took place on April 6, 1875.

42. George Bent makes explicit Cheyenne males' lack of acceptance of the "white man's system of arrest" in Hyde, *Life of George Bent*, 365.

43. Popular accounts recall Black Horse's death. But George Bent makes it clear that he knew Black Horse and that Black Horse lived to be an old man. Ibid., 366.

44. Lieutenant Colonel Thomas Neill to assistant adjutant general, Department of the Missouri, April 7, 1875. The classic Cheyenne source for the Sand Hill fight is George Bent in Hyde, *Life of George Bent*, 365–367. An excellent overview from the military perspective is William H. Leckie, *The Military Conquest of the Southern Plains* (Norman: University of Oklahoma Press, 1963), 231–235.

45. Hyde, *Life of George Bent*, 366.

46. This reconstruction of the Sand Hill fight from the U.S. soldiers' side of the lines was reconstructed from Neill's official report to the adjutant general in Leckie, *The Military Conquest*, 232–233.

47. Hyde, *Life of George Bent*, 366.

48. Powell, *People of the Sacred Mountain*, 2:900.

49. Ibid., 902.

Chapter IV

———

Austin Henely

> I cannot find words to express the courage, patience, endurance,
> and intelligence exhibited by all under my command . . . All the
> men behaved with great gallant[r]y.
>
> —Austin Henely, second lieutenant, 6th Cavalry, on the Battle
> of Sappa Creek, April 26, 1875

One of the 6th Cavalry officers in the field under Colonel Nelson A. Miles's command during operations on the Staked Plains in 1874 was Second Lieutenant Austin Henely. He was a twenty-six-year-old Irish immigrant only two years out of West Point. Little that can be ascertained from the sketchy evidence of Henely's early life would lead anyone to conclude that events of his youth had forged within him the deep-rooted hatred of Indians assumed in some modern accounts of the Sappa Creek fight. If Henely harbored such prejudice because he was himself a victim of discrimination, nothing in the record reveals it.[1]

Austin Henely was born in Ireland in October 1847, apparently to a family of modest means. He immigrated to the United States with his parents at an early age, one of thousands of Irish to escape harsh economic times in Ireland during the 1840s. The Henely family settled for a time on a small farm near Easton, Pennsylvania. There the young Austin grew up along the Delaware River where it forms the border with New Jersey north of Philadelphia, far from the homeland of the Southern Cheyennes. During the Civil War, at age seventeen, Henely enlisted in the regular army, where he served in the 11th Infantry for three years, from September 14, 1864, to September 14, 1867. During that time he won promotion to sergeant of D Company and, later, to regimental quartermaster sergeant.[2]

Apparently his leadership abilities as a noncommissioned officer impressed someone of influence, for within a year of his discharge Henely received an appointment to the United States Military Academy at West Point. He entered the academy in July 1868. His student record at West Point is unrevealing. Apparently he avoided serious trouble. But during his four years as a cadet he was on hospital call twenty-five times for minor ailments ranging from "headaches" to "neuralgia" to "boils." He graduated thirty-fourth in a class of fifty-seven in June 1872.[3]

On June 14 of that year Henely was commissioned a second lieutenant and assigned to the 6th Cavalry. Soon the army ordered him to the Kansas frontier in the Department of the Missouri. His first post was Fort Hays. During the Red River War in 1874, orders took him closer to the action at Fort Dodge. By that time his father had died and his mother, Delia, had married a man named Callihan and moved to Richmond, Virginia. Mr. Callihan lost most of the family's money in Virginia and apparently was in danger of losing his life over a feud precipitated by some local political misfortune. Delia and her husband then moved to Chicago, where Mr. Callihan died. Austin Henely's mother found herself almost destitute and living in a small apartment at 191 South Jefferson Street. From this time (about 1872), she had to rely on a portion of her son's army pay to make ends meet.[4] Whether or not Henely's family problems affected his attitudes and actions in the Red River War is impossible to ascertain.

In August 1874, two battalions of the 6th Cavalry that were organized at Fort Dodge formed part of a wing of Colonel Miles's command that swept across the Staked Plains in pursuit of the warring bands of Indians. Henely served with a scouting expedition that month under Lieutenant Frank Baldwin. The commanded included eighteen troopers of the 6th Cavalry and a number of Delaware Indian scouts. Baldwin and Henely scouted west to Palo Duro Creek, then south to Adobe Walls and down the Canadian River to the Antelope Hills, where they rejoined Miles and the main command.[5]

In December 1874 new orders brought Henely to Fort Lyon, Colorado Territory, one of the westernmost posts in the chain of forts that had ineffectively safeguarded the Arkansas and Smoky Hill valleys during the 1860s. There, in mid-April 1875, Henely received word through department headquarters to leave at once with H Company, 6th Cavalry for Fort Wallace, Kansas, to intercept Little Bull's northward-fleeing people. Reports on April 18 placed the Cheyennes near Punished Woman Creek (White Woman Creek) near modern Scott City, Kansas.[6] In contrast to the army's agonizingly slow responses to the Indian raids around Fort Wallace during the 1860s, troops in 1875 could be mobilized from other posts by telegraph in a matter of minutes. A few hours by rail could bring them to almost any area of Indian activity. Given the speed of rail connections and that by 1875 the Indians were not perceived to be a threat in western Kansas, no cavalry were stationed at Fort Wallace. Consequently, Henely proceeded with haste. We can see from Henely's pursuit that he sensed an opportunity for action under his leadership and perhaps a chance for promotion, an opportunity that was rare for a junior officer on the military frontier.

H Company boarded a branch line of the Kansas Pacific Railroad at the Santa Fe Railroad yards in Las Animas, Colorado Territory, on the evening of April 18. "We were on board, horses and men, by 9 o'clock that evening," Private Marcus M. Robbins remembered. "After a backbreaking ride over a new road for nearly 100 miles, we reached Fort Wallace early the next morning [April 19]. Unloading our horses from the train, we stopped only long enough to feed them and then we started for the hunt."[7]

Indeed, the fleeing Cheyennes were ahead of Henely's troopers when he arrived at Fort Wallace. Several bands had made the dash north after the Sand Hill fight. Besides Little Bull's Suhtai, with twenty lodges, a separate group under Bull Elk had entered Kansas, as had a band of the Aorta people under Sand Hill. With Sand Hill was Black Hairy Dog, the son of the sacred arrow keeper, Medicine Arrows, who already in midwinter had made his escape to the Northern Cheyennes. Medicine Arrows had feared the whites would take *Maahotse* from him if he surrendered, so he took the revered icons north to keep them safe.[8] Shortly before each crossed the Smoky Hill Road the bands came together, and there the soldiers first picked up their trail.

Meanwhile, at Darlington Agency, Lieutenant Colonel Neill reported to department headquarters that:

> When the Indians left the Sand-hills they went west up the North Fork of the Canadian, and joined those who had not surrendered [Little Bull's band]; the latter were on the road to the agency to surrender when the fight commenced. I judge the total number of Cheyennes out to be 200 or perhaps 250. They have stolen near 100 head of stock from here, and those who were coming in [Little Bull] probably have a thousand ponies.* [9]

With Henely when he began his pursuit from Fort Wallace on the morning of April 19 was Second Lieutenant C. C. Hewitt, 19th Infantry, the officer who had recovered the bodies of the John German family. Hewitt kept the official log of the march with not much more than a simple compass. Acting Assistant Surgeon F. H. Atkins accompanied the command, along with Mr. Homer Wheeler, a part-time rancher and the post trader at Fort Wallace. Wheeler knew the area well and was taken along as guide and scout. The command had fifteen days' rations and ten days' forage transported in wagons drawn by two teams of six mules each.

H Company struck out from Fort Wallace to find the Cheyenne but could only make thirteen miles by nightfall. On the morning of April 20 Henely sent his baggage wagons back to Hackberry Creek and continued the pursuit. Soon Corporal William W. Morris discovered the trail of about twelve lodges around noon. Henely abandoned half of his equipage and

---

* Neill's report that Little Bull's band was coming in to surrender conflicts somewhat with Bent's assertion that Little Bull had made his mind up not to surrender and was waiting to make an escape north. Bent, however (or perhaps it was Hyde's editing), likewise contradicts himself in the same passage by asserting that Little Bull was coming in to the agency at the time. See Hyde, *Life of George Bent*, 367. Neill's assertion that Little Bull possessed a herd of a thousand ponies was probably greatly overestimated.

forage and began a forced march to the Smoky Hill River. On the dark night of April 21, the command followed a rain-soaked trail across the tracks of the Kansas Pacific Railroad near Monument Station. There the trail split, and Henely followed the branch to the northwest but eventually lost it altogether.[10] This was probably the trail of the band led by the Southern Cheyenne Spotted Wolf. Little Bull's combined band split shortly after crossing the Smoky Hill River, where the Indians discovered that the soldiers were on their trail. Spotted Wolf struck out to the northwest whereas Little Bull, with only a portion of his Suhtai, struck northeast. Sand Hill, probably his son, Yellow Horse, and Black Hairy Dog, along with a few of the Aortas, followed Little Bull. Bull Elk's people, if they ever had joined with Little Bull below the Smoky Hill, probably followed Spotted Wolf. In any event, according to the Cheyennes, it was Spotted Wolf's party that Henely followed for a time between the Smoky Hill and Solomon Rivers.[11]

After losing the Indian trail, Henely headed for the headwaters of the Solomon River, where the command bivouacked on the night of April 21. After consulting with Wheeler and Hewitt, Henely decided to move to the northeast. He headed toward the old Cheyenne and Lakota hunting sites along the North Fork of Beaver Creek in Republican River country where, he reasoned, the Indians would hunt for food and rest for the night before moving on toward the northern agencies across the Nebraska border. The Cheyennes, it seemed, had eluded him.

But fortune favored Henely. Shortly after daylight on April 22, his command met a party of buffalo hunters who complained the Indians had robbed their base camp while they were away hunting. The hunters, fearing an outbreak from the reservation, told Henely they were headed south to the safety of Fort Wallace. They informed Henely that the Indian trail he had picked up probably led to the Middle Fork of Sappa Creek, about seventeen miles to the north. Three of the hunters, Henry Campbell, Charles Schroeder, and Samuel B. Srach, volunteered to guide the command to the vicinity of the supposed Cheyenne camp. Again the anxious Henely sensed opportunity. The command moved out at once, accompanied by the three hunters. They rode a distance of six miles, where Henely's command bivouacked unseen in a ravine until nightfall and then marched to within five miles of the Sappa. There H Company waited for dawn.[12]

By now Henely, although he did not realize it, was hot on the trail of Little Bull's people. According to the Cheyennes, some of Spotted Wolf's scouts saw Henely's command move off to the northeast. Accordingly, Spotted Wolf sent a warrior named Chicken Hawk to warn Little Bull that soldiers were on his trail. Chicken Hawk had some relatives in Little Bull's band and wished to warn them of impending danger. Unfortunately, Chicken Hawk's horse was in such bad shape that he was not able to get between the soldiers and Little Bull's band in order to warn Little Bull.[13]

Because Homer Wheeler and the three hunters knew the country better than anyone in the command, Henely sent the four civilians ahead to scout the Sappa for the location of any Cheyenne encampment. The men started out on black horses so as to be less likely to be discovered in the darkness by Indian wolves. Soon they approached the Middle Fork of the Sappa.[14] A row of white alkali flats at first deceived the men because they looked like tepees in the overcast night. The four rode downstream (to the northeast) and again saw what appeared to be tepees. These turned out to be old buffalo wallows on a hillside. At that point the hunters figured the Indians were not on the Sappa at all, but Wheeler remained determined to push on downstream. "I asked them how far it was to timber," he remembered, "and they said about twelve miles. I told them the chances were that the Indians had struck for shelter, as it was cold and disagreeable, and I suggested we ride on . . . but they refused, so I started off alone. After riding some distance I discovered that they [the three hunters] were following me and felt better."[15]

Eventually the moon came out, and Wheeler discovered fresh horse droppings. The men followed the trail to discover if it led to a camp or was left by a herd of wild horses, abundant then in northwest Kansas. "At last I rode up a ridge and carefully looked over the top," Wheeler wrote years later. "Here I saw some horses in the bend of the river. At first I thought they were wild horses but soon found I was mistaken, for they had seen me and did not seem frightened."[16]

Soon the hunters came up and looked out over the ridge into the darkness. "Holy smoke," one of them exclaimed. "There they are."[17]

The scouts rode away quietly and arrived back at camp about 2:00 A.M. on April 23. Immediately Lieutenant Henely ordered his command to boots and saddles. With Wheeler as guide, the command set off north in the direction of the Middle Fork of Sappa Creek. They arrived there in the gray light of dawn. Wheeler located the pony herd once again and then the Cheyenne camp a few hundred yards below. "Mr. Wheeler . . . galloped furiously back," Henely remembered, "swinging his hat and shouting at the top of his voice. I immediately galloped toward him with my command, and the camp was displayed to view."[18]

Earlier, a few of the Indians had apparently rounded up some of the ponies. But Henely and Wheeler saw no Inidans who might have sounded an alarm. "Three or four of the tepees were old and nearly the color of dead grass," Wheeler remembered. "I did not see them until quite near. No one was stirring in the camp; not even the dogs had given the alarm as they usually do when prowlers are around."[19]

"Crawling to the edge of the bluffs we were rewarded by a full view of their camp," Private Marcus M. Robbins remembered, "with the entire herd of nearly 400 animals a half mile away and no one guarding."[20] Henely's command, it seemed, had caught Little Bull's sleeping camp by surprise.

Notes

1. 6-1877. Appointment, Commission and Personal file, Austin Henely, Rg 94, AGO/NARA, File 3490-1874. Microform. (Hereafter referred to as "Henely's ACP File").

2. Constance Wynn Altshuler, ed., *Cavalry Yellow and Infantry Blue: Army Officers in Arizona Between 1851 and 1886* (Tucson: Arizona Historical Society, 1991), 164.

3. Henely's ACP File.

4. Mrs. Delia Callihan to adjutant general's office, August 4, 1878, letter in Henely's ACP File.

5. Haley, *The Buffalo War*, 174; Powell, *People of the Sacred Mountain*, 2:864–865; Johnson, "Austin Henely," 11.

6. Henely's ACP File; Henely's Report, 89.

7. "Chasing Indians by Railroad: Marcus M. Robbins," in Beyer and Keydel, *Deeds of Valor*, 1:198 (hereafter referred to as "Robbins's Account"). An account of Robbins's exploits was also

published in 1906 by Will Kenyon, "The Last Raid of Spotted Horse," *Sunday Magazine,* August 12, 1906. The account is full of errors and embellishments and was even criticized by F. M. Lockard, an amusing case of someone living in a glass house throwing bricks. The Spotted Horse Kenyon writes about is probably fictitious and not the Spotted Horse renowned in the 1860s.

8. Although Sandoz in *Cheyenne Autumn* declares Medicine Arrows was one of the Sappa Creek casualties, she is mistaken. Over the years Cheyenne historian Peter John Powell has gone to great lengths to demonstrate that Medicine Arrows escaped north in the winter of 1874–1875 and was not with Little Bull's band at Sappa Creek that spring. See George Bent to George Hyde, September 5, 1914, May 11, 1915, and May 11, 1917, Bent-Hyde Correspondence, Coe Collection, Yale University Library; Powell, *People of the Sacred Mountain,* 2:895–896; and Powell, *Sweet Medicine,* 2:866–867

9. House, *Report of the Secretary of War for the Year 1875,* 88.

10. Henely's Report, 89.

11. George Bent in Hyde, *Life of George Bent,* 367–368.

12. Henely's Report, 89. For the most complete geographical accounting of both Henely's and Little Bull's movements from Indian Territory to Sappa Creek in relation to both modern and nineteenth-century landmarks see Chalfant, *Cheyennes at Dark Water Creek,* 60–105.

13. George Bent in Hyde, *Life of George Bent,* 367–368.

14. Wheeler claimed it was the North Fork. Like Henely, he probably was ignorant of the small North Fork. Nevertheless, the most complete account of the approach to and discovery of Little Bull's camp is Wheeler's. He published two almost identical versions in Homer W. Wheeler, *Buffalo Days,* (Indianapolis: Bobbs-Merrill, 1925), 102–104 and *The Frontier Trail: A Personal Narrative by Col. Homer W. Wheeler, Famous Frontiersman* (Los Angeles: Times-Mirror Press, 1923), 143–146.

15. Wheeler, *Buffalo Days,* 102–103.

16. Ibid., 103.

17. Ibid.

18. Henely's Report, 90.

19. Wheeler, *Buffalo Days,* 104.

20. Robbins's Account, 198.

Colonel Nelson A. Miles near the end of his military service. Miles began his illustrious military career in the West in 1874–1875 during the Red River War. Courtesy, Kansas State Historical Society.

Seventeen-year-old Catherine German shortly after her release by the Cheyennes. Courtesy, Kansas State Historical Society.

Twelve-year-old Sophia German shortly after her release by the Cheyennes. Courtesy, Kansas State Historical Society.

Left, five-year-old Adelaide German and seven-year-old Julia German as photographed at Fort Leavenworth, Kansas, about six weeks after their rescue by the U.S. Army. Colonel Nelson A. Miles sent this photograph to Catherine while she was still a captive of the Cheyennes. Courtesy, Kansas State Historical Society.

Second Lieutenant Austin Henely as a cadet at West Point. Years later, Henely became an enigma for his role in the tragic encounter with Little Bull's party of Southern Cheyennes at Sappa Creek on April 23, 1875. Courtesy, Kansas State Historical Society.

Homer Wheeler after he entered military service. Wheeler was a civilian at the time of the Sappa Creek Massacre. His knowledge of the western Kansas plains was crucial to the 6th Cavalry in locating Little Bull's Cheyennes after they moved north from Indian Territory in a fatal attempt to find refuge among the Northern Cheyennes. Wheeler left one of the most important accounts of the Sappa Creek incident in his memoirs. Courtesy, Kansas State Historical Society.

Renditions of Fort Wallace, Kansas, frequently appeared in *Harper's Weekly* during the late 1860s, when the fort was one of the most besieged outposts on the western military frontier. By the time of the Red River War in 1874–1875, no cavalry detachments were stationed at Fort Wallace. In April 1875, Company H, 6th Cavalry from Fort Lyon had to travel to the post by rail from Kit Carson, Colorado Territory, before they could begin their pursuit northward to intercept the Cheyennes that had fled from Indian Territory. Courtesy, Kansas State Historical Society.

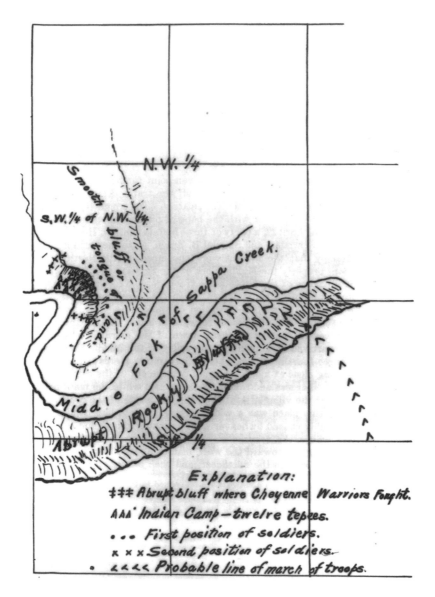

Explanation:
‡‡‡ Abrupt bluff where Cheyenne Warriors Fought.
ᴧᴧᴧ Indian Camp—twelve tepees.
••• First position of soldiers.
х х х Second position of soldiers.
• ᴧᴧᴧᴧ Probable line of march of troops.

William D. Street's map of the Sappa Creek battlefield. Although Street, an early homesteader near Oberlin, Kansas, was not a participant in the attack on Little Bull's camp, he became fascinated with the incident and drew a map of the battlefield for publication in the *Kansas Historical Collections* for 1907–1908. Although it contains errors as to the precise point of attack and troop positioning, the map conforms well logistically to the pattern of engagement. Courtesy, Kansas State Historical Society.

Amache Ochinee Prowers, or Walking Woman, as she was known among the Cheyenne, was married to the prominent Arkansas Valley rancher John W. Prowers. When she saw at Fort Lyon, Colorado Territory, that the war bonnet of the sacred-arrow keeper, Stone Forehead, had been taken as a war trophy at Sappa Creek, she foretold death for Lieutenant Austin Henely within a year. Although his death came in almost three years, Henely drowned in a flash flood in Arizona Territory in 1878 while stationed at Fort Bowie. Stone Forehead was not present at Sappa Creek, but Amache Prowers's assumption that he was probably led Mari Sandoz to assert in *Cheyenne Autumn* that the esteemed arrow keeper had died in Little Bull's village. Courtesy, Colorado Historical Society.

George Bent and his wife, Magpie. George Bent was the son of trader William Bent and Owl Woman, a Southern Cheyenne. George Bent's wife, Magpie, was a niece of the great Southern Cheyenne peace chief Black Kettle, a victim of the Sand Creek Massacre and casualty at Washita. George Bent rode with the Dog Soldiers in their raids following Sand Creek and went to the reservation with the Cheyennes, where he lived until 1918. In his later years he interviewed aging warriors and wrote a history of the Cheyenne people in a series of letters to ethnologist George Hyde, who assembled them in a book-length manuscript. Discovered and published in 1964 by Savoie Lottinville, Bent's account of Sappa Creek (at which he was not present) stood in contrast to earlier accounts of the event. Bent gives us the only reliable Cheyenne account of the affair, a viewpoint unknown to earlier white interpreters of the battle. Courtesy, Colorado Historical Society.

An early homesteader in northwest Kansas, William D. Street lived near Cheyenne Hole, site of the Sappa Creek Massacre. Street became fascinated with the incident and visited the site frequently. His 1908 account of that fight, ostensibly based on information from white participants, was the basis on which later writers, including Mari Sandoz, accused Lieutenant Austin Henely of leading a massacre at Sappa Creek. Courtesy, Kansas State Historical Society.

Not to be outdone by William D. Street, F. M. Lockard, another early resident of northwest Kansas and later a district judge, wrote an account of the Sappa Creek affair in 1909 alleging that atrocities had been committed by the 6th Cavalry. Lockard, who was not at Sappa Creek, also claimed to have intimate knowledge of the fight from participants. But his account is full of errors, based in part on earlier completely erroneous accounts and in part on Street's account. But Lockard's and Street's accounts together dramatically contradict Lieutenant Henely's official report to the adjutant general of the army and gave impetus to the massacre thesis. They have been widely cited by writers interpreting the Sappa Creek Massacre within the contexts of evolving intellectual and political attitudes through the years. Courtesy, Kansas State Historical Society.

Chapter V

The Battle of Sappa Creek

The troops attacked at daybreak of April 23, 1875, taking the Cheyennes by surprise, though a number got away over the bluffs to the pony herds.[From the rifle pits] the hostiles gave us a hot reception, the man who had the temerity to poke his head over the bank getting it—literally—"in the neck."

—Private Marcus M. Robbins

The secluded bend on the middle Sappa where Little Bull's people stopped to rest soon came to be called Cheyenne Hole by settlers. For years in Rawlins County, the name possessed brooding connotations. George Bent later described it as "a good place in which to hide, but a poor one to defend in a fight . . ."[1] At this point in their journey north, Little Bull's band consisted of about twelve lodges, or approximately sixty people including women and children.* But there may have been a few more, because Henely's men later discovered what he described as "sleeping holes" that had been dug into natural depressions in the bluffs above the stream and presumably used by some of the Indians who had no lodges.[2] The camp was tucked below some rugged bluffs that rose above the northwest bank of Sappa

---

* Both Bent's informants and the military records agree on the estimate of twelve lodges.

Creek. These bluffs were part of a tongue of land formed where the stream made a sharp horseshoe bend along marshy ground. This terrain was difficult to cross in an attack of the camp from the west side, where the Indians could not see the soldiers. On the smooth plateau above the camp the Indian ponies grazed contentedly, unaware of impending danger. Along the south bank of the creek were some abrupt rocky bluffs, on which H Company awaited instructions from their lieutenant.[3]

Henely ordered Sergeant George Kitchen and ten men to cross the stream and surround the bulk of the pony herd, kill the herders, and round up as many horses as possible that were grazing close to the main command. Five men then would secure the herd while the remaining five would rejoin the body of H Company in the attack. "With the rest of my command," Henely reported, "I intended to intrude myself between the Indians and their herd and attack them if they did not surrender."[4]

Henely's tactics were in no way unusual. For more than a decade experience had taught the army that a surprise attack on a camp at dawn was the most reliable way to keep the Indians from scattering. By destroying the camp, the army would deprive the enemy of food and supplies necessary to continue their existence away from the reservation. But too often noncombatant women and children were present and unavoidably joined the casualty lists. By 1875 total war had become a reality in white-Indian combat on the Great Plains.

As the morning light began to gather strength over the Sappa valley, the soldiers were discovered. "Hearing a slight noise," Homer Wheeler remembered, "I looked around and saw, not more than two hundred yards away, an Indian herder running for dear life to notify the camp of the approach of enemies. The Indians were instantly stirring and I saw them pour from their tepees as I started to warn the lieutenant."[5] Henely immediately ordered the advance. Flowing in a northeasterly direction, Sappa Creek carved a deep horseshoe bend that made the attack even more difficult than originally anticipated. The banks were boggy, and only with effort were Henely and Wheeler able to move through the mud. "I plunged in with my horse," Henely recalled, "Mr. Wheeler with me. By extraordinary efforts our horses floundered through."[6] The command was reluctant to follow, but Henely urged them on. 'We have crossed,' Wheeler heard Henely say. 'Now every man of you must cross.' The troopers then rode in without further hesitation," Wheeler wrote, "and after much floundering all crossed safely, although one man lost his carbine and another his pistol."[7]

"The Indian camp suddenly came to life," Sergeant Fred Platten remembered. "Indians streamed out of their tepees and wanted to know what we wanted. Through an interpreter the lieutenant told them to surrender as prisoners and they would be treated well." The Cheyennes, "in turn demanded that we give back their horses . . ."[8]

"It was a complete surprise," Private Marcus M. Robbins remembered.[9] "We moved up and ordered the Indians to surrender," Wheeler added, "making signs which they well understood. One warrior said in pretty good English, 'Go away, John; bring back our ponies.' They then fired on us and the fun commenced."[10]

Henely remembered no verbal response from the Indians. "I gave the command to fight on foot," he reported, "which was obeyed with extraordinary promptness . . . I then ordered my men to fire and posted them around the crest in skirmish line."[11]

Little Bull's surprised camp had little chance to resist effectively. "The troops rushed across the creek and took up a position where they could pour a cross fire into the Indians," Cheyenne informants conveyed to George Bent. "The long-range guns of the buffalo hunters did much execution, and though the Indians put up a stiff fight they suffered severely."[*][12] Sergeant Platten remembered the Indians opening fire on the troops as they crossed the creek. "Most of us were still in the creek [when the firing started]," he wrote. "I was off my horse, trying to lead him out, when I was struck a glancing blow on the back of my neck by an arrow; it didn't hurt much, however, except my feelings."[13]

---

* Several white writers who were not at the scene, most notably Mari Sandoz, have made much of the killing effect of the .50 caliber weapons wielded by the civilians in this fight. None of the eyewitness military accounts mentions the effectiveness of the weapons, although Henely in his official report acknowledged the services of the civilians in dispersing the pony herd above the bluffs.

Homer Wheeler likewise vividly recalled the first fusillade: "I must have been greatly excited, for I remember little of what was going on during the next few minutes. When I recovered my senses I was lying on the ground, pumping lead into the Indians. It was hand to hand conflict."[14]

Private Marcus M. Robbins remembered the attack as devastating,

and all who were not killed at the first charge, or made their escape, took refuge in the natural rifle pits along the bank of the stream, made by the washouts at high water. In these pits, the hostiles gave us a hot reception, the man who had the temerity to poke his head over the bank getting it—literally— "in the neck." We lost two men in this manner in as many minutes.[15]

The only casualties suffered by H Company, 6th Cavalry that day were two in number. They were Sergeant Theodore Papier and Private Robert Theims. The troopers were both killed instantly from an exposed position not more than fifteen or twenty feet from the Cheyenne camp. According to Henely, they were "fighting with extraordinary courage" when they fell.[16] But Sergeant Platten remembered that the two soldiers "became confused and broke ranks to charge the enemy. They were the immediate target of a dozen Indians."[17] "Themis [sic] was our cook," Homer Wheeler recalled years later, "and was supposed to remain with the wagon . . . Poor fellow, he lost his life by not obeying instructions."[18]

Following the return of H Company to Fort Wallace, the bodies of the two troopers, both of German descent and "well liked among the men," were buried with full military honors at Fort Wallace. Later they were reinterred at Fort Leavenworth, the last enlisted men to be killed in action during the Indian wars in Kansas.*[19]

---

* The last officer to lose his life during the Indian wars in Kansas was Colonel W. H. Lewis, 19th Infantry, who died in October 1878 of wounds suffered in the Battle of Punished Woman's Fork. The army was in pursuit of Dull Knife's and Little Wolf's bands of Northern Cheyennes, which had recently left Darlington Agency to return to their homelands on the northern plains. General Sheridan reported one enlisted man killed in Kansas on September 27, 1878, at the Battle of Punished Woman's Fork. But firsthand records indicate that Sheridan was mistaken.

But the Cheyennes remembered the death of one of these men (probably Sergeant Papier) quite differently. In testimony given to George Bent years later (probably by Blind Bull), "so many of the women and children were killed and wounded [in the initial attack] that Little Bull and Dirty Water went out to parley with the soldiers. A sergeant [Sergeant Papier] came out to meet them." But a warrior named "White Bear, [stepson of Black Hairy Dog] from his position near the creek bed, shot and killed the sergeant . . . Blind Bull told me." Bent confessed "that he could not understand why White Bear killed the sergeant. This killing caused Little Bull and Dirty Water, an old man, to be shot down. For some time after the killing of the sergeant the troops kept up a hot fire on the Indians and finally turned off in the direction taken by those who had escaped at the opening of the fight."[20]

The Cheyenne account of the Sappa Creek fight was not discovered and published until 1968. As such, it was not available to Mari Sandoz in 1953 when she reconstructed the battle's events in Cheyenne Autumn. Apparently G. Derek West was also unaware of Bent's memoir when he published his article on Sappa Creek in 1968. The only military source that mentions a possible attempt to parley is Henely's official report, and then only briefly and inconclusively. "One Indian, who appeared to be a chief," Henely wrote, "made some rapid gesticulations, which I at first thought was for a parley, but soon discovered it was directed toward those in the rear."[21]

Henely wrote this statement, however, prior to his description of the commencement of the attack, and not after many casualties had been suffered among the Cheyenne, as Bent states. Quite possibly Henely was confused about when the event transpired. Perhaps he could not clearly see the aborted parley from his position in the line. In his report Henely writes that the line of fire between the two sides was somewhat complex and obscured by the configuration of the terrain. "If we imagine the dress-circle of a theater to be lowered to within about five feet of the pit," he wrote, "the men to be deployed about the edge and the Indians down among the orchestra chairs; it will give some idea of our relative positions. The most exposed part was near the center of the arc, corresponding to that part of the dress-circle opposite the entrance."[22]

Whether or not Henely was close to Papier and Theims when they were killed is impossible to ascertain; he only reported that they appeared to be about fifteen or twenty feet away from the Indians. From his description of the obscured line of fire and the likelihood of events transpiring rapidly, Henely might not have been able to tell what exactly was going on at the time Bent asserts that White Bear broke the supposed truce. If Bent is correct in his admission of White Bear's blunder, Henely in no way would have been reluctant to relate the incident in his official report if he had witnessed it personally. If the event was related to him later by any of his men, perhaps he thought it prudent not to report such an important incident based on hearsay, even if corroborated, because he had not personally witnessed it. In all likelihood, his mention of what appeared to be a parley possibly was a parley, given that the sequence of events moved rapidly and led to White Bear's killing of the sergeant as Bent relates.

Immediately after the alleged parley, the troopers were overcome with a sort of frenzy for the next "twenty minutes,"[23] as Private Marcus M. Robbins described it, to "rout the rascals out of their holes . . ."[24] For among those Cheyennes who did not escape, H Company took no prisoners. According to one turn-of-the-century source, "the shibboleth of the troopers was 'Remember the Germaine [sic] Family' . . ."[25] If we accept the Indian account of the battle, certainly White Bear's disregard for any kind of temporary truce, combined with memories of the sensational propaganda of the German massacre, would explain the "frenzied" fighting by the troopers, who took no prisoners, and the complete destruction of Little Bull's camp that followed.

"The Indians fell like ten-pins," Sergeant Platten recalled of this time. "When they rose up to shoot . . . they were shot down. Our six-shooters were far superior to their rifles and bows and arrows, for close fighting."[26] As the soldiers approached the Cheyenne's rifle pits, the fighting continued at close quarters. What was left of Little Bull's band did not give up, preferring instead to die as warriors even as their ammunition ran short. "One of the Indians reached over the [stream] bank and secured one of the trooper's guns, and used it against us," Wheeler remembered. "The lieutenant had some trouble in getting his men to lie down. They fought like madmen. Their whole desire seemed to be to charge the Indians and drive them out . . . It seemed as if we never would drive them out. Some of them hid behind the creek bank and the men could only see them when they raised their heads to shoot."[27]

One pocket of Cheyenne fighting men was obscured from view, so Henely ordered a flanking movement to achieve a more direct line of fire. Marcus M. Robbins, a private, claimed he led the maneuver. "Taking four or five men with me," he recalled years later,

> we made a detour down to the creek until out of sight of the hostiles; then getting into the creek, we waded in the mud and water back up the stream until directly behind the rifle pits, doing this without attracting the attention of the Indians. Then making the signal agreed upon, we sprang up the bank directly into the pit, while the rest charged from above at the same time . . . I had run my head into many a "hornet's nest" in my time but they did not compare with that which buzzed around us for a while. I still have a hazy recollection of emptying my revolver into an Indian who sprang up in front of me, and of my "bunkie" saying I had saved his life, but how I did it is impossible for me to tell, so frenzied in "battle fever" was I at the time.

For actions unspecified by Henely as to particular details, Private Marcus M. Robbins won the Medal of Honor for heroism at Sappa Creek.[28]

Meanwhile, Homer Wheeler also advanced to a better position.

> I went around to the rear, unnoticed by them, but to do this [I] had to crawl some distance on my hands and knees through the grass. From my new position I could see the Indians lying along the bank, and I soon drove them from this position. As soon as they had discovered me they all commenced firing on me and made it mighty uncomfortable, and I was not slow to leave my dangerous position. I had to run the gauntlet for some fifty yards, in order to reach a place of safety. I ran in a zigzag manner, falling down two or three times, which no doubt saved me, as the bullets whistled around me as thick as bees when swarming.

Eventually Wheeler joined one of the detachments of skirmishers and "volunteered to lead a charge" on the rifle pits.[29]

After about twenty furious minutes of this close-quarter fighting a lull occurred from the Cheyenne position. Concluding all were dead, Lieutenant Henely ordered his men to mount and pursue those Indians who had earlier escaped to the pony herd. "Hardly had we mounted," Henely reported,

> when two Indians ran up to the two bodies [Papier and Theims] . . . I immediately detached three or four men at a gallop to charge them, and the Indians retreated, accomplishing nothing. Just then an Indian, gaudily decked, jumped from a hole, and with peculiar side-long leaps [Henely did not suppose a reason for this behavior], attempted to escape, which he did not.[30]

This man might have been White Bear, the warrior who broke the truce and brought about the final onslaught. Years later, Blind Bull, who escaped along with White Bear's stepfather, Black Hairy Dog, told George Bent that, "as the troopers started away, White Bear rose up and fired at them. They turned and shot [White Bear] and he fell into the creek."[31]

The fighting had almost ended. "Seeing a herd of ponies on the hill beside me," Henely wrote of this point in the fight, "I sent two men to bring them in. A number of Indians tried to cut them off. I mounted and went to their assistance, driving the Indians off and bringing in the herd. Coming back . . . a solitary shot was fired from the holes, striking the horse of Trumpeter [Michael] Dawson through the body. I then concluded to make a sure finish—."[32] Henely ordered Corporal William W. Morris to take "a detachment to advance to the edge of the crest," telling them to keep up "a continual fire" while "another detachment went to the left and rear, and advanced together."[33]

The men of H Company overran the Cheyenne's rifle pits with a final rush and captured the camp. "When we arrived at the rifle pits," Wheeler vividly recalled,

> a big Indian jumped out of one of the holes and fired at us, the ball passing through my cartridge box. A young soldier, a mere boy, and I ran

after him. The soldier was several feet in advance of me, firing at the Indian with his six-shooter. He emptied it as the Indian dropped down behind a little ridge and took dead aim at the soldier. Throwing up my gun, I "beat the Indian to it," and shot him through the head, killing him instantly.

The young soldier grasped Wheeler's hand and, with tears in his eyes, thanked him "for saving his life." Wheeler claimed this was the last Indian he saw killed in the final assault on the rifle pits. The warrior had a three-banded Springfield rifle, which Wheeler remembered was "half cocked, and a cartridge was in the chamber. I shot so quickly that the Indian did not have time to pull the trigger.* [34]

"When every Indian in sight was slain," Sergeant Platten remembered,

we poked around through the tepees looking for more. While thus engaged, an Indian came boldly into the center of the camp, riding one horse and leading another. We were so dumb-founded at the foolhardy stunt that he rode in, jumped off his horse, and lifted up a buffalo robe from the ground before we came out of our trance. Out from under the robe, jumped an Indian. Both Indians leaped on the horses and raced off. A well placed rifle bullet caused the Indian who had so boldly come in to our camp to fold up and roll off his horse, dead, but the other raced on, unhit.[35]

A warrior named Little Bear, who was one of those who made an escape to the pony herd, probably committed this suicidal act. "After catching his pony," Blind Bull told George Bent years later, "he suddenly announced to his companions that he would ride back to the gully where the Indians were fighting. Little Bear went back and charged into the troops and was killed." When Bent inquired why Little Bear had done this thing, Blind Bull told him that Little Bear's "father and mother had also been killed here earlier in the fight." Six months later, Little Bear's horse was found by a party

---

* Wheeler here may be describing the same event, the killing of White Bear, that Henely earlier described.

of Arapahos on the North Fork of the Canadian River, far from the site of its owner's death.[36]

Sergeant Platten chased off after the unknown warrior who had escaped as a result of Little Bear's defiant act.* "Back I went, on the run," Platten recounted. Soon, however, he discovered that a companion had joined the fleeing warrior. "It was too late to turn back," Platten recalled,

> so I charged them both on foot with my rifle in one hand and my six-shooter in the other. An arrow whizzed past my ear, so I thought I'd better do something and quick. The most dangerous looking of the two was the one with the rifle. I slowed up a little to aim the six-shooter and shot and killed him. The other turned and ran. I stopped, brought up my rifle, and at a range of about 100 yards killed the fleeing Indian.[37]

Platten's boast seems unlikely. Presumably, however, one or more members of H Company witnessed some of Platten's actions that day, for the United States awarded him the Medal of Honor for valor at the Battle of Sappa Creek.

The guns fell silent shortly after the final assault on the rifle pits. "The contest was over," Private Marcus M. Robbins recalled, "for there were no more foes to fight."[38] In his official report, Lieutenant Henely stated that the battle lasted about three hours. He listed two members of H Company killed (Sergeant Papier and Private Theims) and none wounded. He reported twenty-seven Cheyennes killed, "nineteen dead warriors . . . eight squaws and children were unavoidably killed by shots intended for the warriors."[39] If we assume the estimate of sixty or more Cheyennes of various ages in the camp, we must conclude that a minimum of thirty-three Cheyennes (more than half the camp) made their way to the pony herd and successfully escaped. Although an early settler in the vicinity, William D. Street, asserted he found

---

* Platten's account becomes confused here. Relating these deeds years later through Thomas Way, Platten supposedly remembered going after one of the warriors who had earlier attempted to scalp Papier's and Theims's corpses. Platten's memory thus does not coincide with Henely's report, written days after the battle. In any event, Platten's claim might have been embellished or fabricated for dramatic effect, either by himself or Thomas Way.

skeletal evidence of seventy bodies, the bones were scattered, and Street's claim (he was neither a physician nor a forensics expert) are highly suspect.[40] Henely also reported that Little Bull's warriors were armed with "rifles and carbines, the Spencer carbine predominating. A number of muzzle-loading rifles, and one Springfield breech-loading, rifle, musket-caliber .50 were found." The army captured 134 horses.[41]

Almost universally in the annals of the Indian wars, casualty figures offered by Indian sources differ widely from official military casualty reports. Amazingly, for the Battle of Sappa Creek George Bent's informants reported twenty-seven casualties, the exact number reported by Henely. The difference, however, is that Bent reported seven warriors and twenty women and children killed, almost the complete reverse of Henely's nineteen warriors and eight women and children killed. According to the Indians, the warriors who lost their lives at the Battle of Sappa Creek were Little Bull (leader of the band), Tangle Hair, Dirty Water, The Rat, White Bear (who brought about catastrophe by killing Sergeant Papier), Young Bear, and Stone Teeth. Bent mentions the name of one woman casualty, Yellow Body Woman, "who was killed in the Gully."

According to known Cheyenne sources, none of the Indian dead at Sappa Creek had ridden with Medicine Water's Bowstrings the previous year, at the time of the Lone Tree and German massacres. Among those who escaped at various times during the fighting were Blind Bull, Bent's principal source for the Sappa Creek fight, who must have escaped late in the action; Black Hairy Dog, later the keeper of the sacred medicine arrows, son of Stone Forehead; Black Hairy Dog's wife, who was the mother of White Bear, killed at Sappa Creek; and presumably, Council Chief Sand Hill. Bent also reported Yellow Horse, Sand Hill's son, as having escaped. Yellow Horse had ridden with Medicine Water's band in Kansas in 1874, but his exact role, if any, in the Lone Tree and German massacres is unknown.[42] How many of the escaped Indians remained in the vicinity, hid, and possibly witnessed the final destruction of the camp is likewise unknown.

Henely reported no wounded among the Cheyenne casualties, but of course Henely took no prisoners. That fact would later haunt Henely's reputation when charges of massacre and the murder of helpless noncombatants were leveled against him by both reputable and nonreputable sources for more than a century following the Battle of Sappa Creek. The events that transpired after the fighting, when Henely's men plundered and burned Little Bull's camp, a common practice during the Indian campaigns of the 1870s, constitute the seeds from which grew the Sappa Creek controversy. The differing speculation over what actually occurred during this time, and what did not, brought about the controversy and insured that it would endure to the present day. "I then burned all their lodges and effects and threw some of the arms into the fire, destroying also a quantity of ammunition," Henely reported.[43]

During this time a confrontation occurred between Lieutenant Henely and Sergeant Frederick Platten, who only a short time before had performed some act of gallantry that would win him a Medal of Honor. "As was customary after a battle of this kind," Platten related years later,

> the lieutenant gave orders to burn the camp, but first we were allowed to pick up any souvenirs we wanted. I entered the supposedly deserted tepee with the lieutenant to look around, a blanket moved on the dirt floor and out crawled a squaw with a papoose under one arm. The other arm had been *shot off* [emphasis mine—probably, if Platten's story is true, by a .50 caliber buffalo rifle] by a stray bullet in the fight.
>
> When Lieutenant Hanley [sic] saw them he ordered that they both be shot. In fact he ordered me to shoot them and toss them in a nearby tepee that was burning. Right then was the only time I ever remember talking back to an officer.
>
> "I've never shot babies and women that I know of," I informed the lieutenant. "and I'm not going to start now."
>
> I have been talked to and about many times, but never had I listened to a dressing-down like that the lieutenant gave me then and there. Somewhere in his tirade I was court-martialed and sentenced to be shot.
>
> Fortunately his anger didn't last long and I was again in the good graces of the troop before the day was over. The lieutenant called in two troopers who were of the opinion that a good Indian was a dead Indian whether buck, squaw or papoose. The squaw and papoose were summarily disposed of, but not by me.[44]

Nowhere in his official report did Henely mention or allude to any kind of displeasure with Platten. Court-martial charges were never filed. Neither Wheeler nor Robbins, the other two white eyewitnesses to the Battle of Sappa Creek who left written records, mentions the intentional killing of any noncombatants. Platten's assertion that Henely threatened to court-martial him is highly suspect. Henely certainly did not hesitate to recommend Platten for the Medal of Honor. Was Henely's recommendation for a decoration genuine or designed to silence Platten? Given the late date at which Platten's story became known—with the publication of his account by Thomas E. Way in 1959—the award seems either to have kept him quiet or, more probably, the incident never occurred. Platten did not receive official notification of his medal until November 14, 1927. This episode in Platten's account suggests embellishment and raises questions. When did Platten relate this experience to Thomas E. Way? Who first wrote the story, Platten or Way? Platten died in 1939; Way published Platten's story in 1959. Was Way familiar with Mari Sandoz's version of the Sappa Creek episode, published six years earlier?

Interestingly, the only contemporary Cheyenne source, George Bent, makes no mention of noncombatant women and children being murdered in the camp after the fighting had ceased. It is possible but doubtful that Bent's editor, George Hyde, excised such accusations from the original manuscript, because unless Hyde destroyed them, there are no original letters from Bent to Hyde supporting the murder of noncombatants.

Of course, unless Blind Bull were hiding nearby, there was no way he could have witnessed atrocities committed following the fight. In any event, years later, Cheyenne oral tradition incorporated the atrocity thesis. Cheyenne historian Father Peter John Powell states that "Jay Black Kettle, then Keeper of Maahotse; Henry Little Coyote, then Keeper of Esevone; Weasel Woman, his wife; John Stands in Timber; and Ralph Whitetail all recalled these acts of brutality, to [Powell personally in] 1959–1961."[45] Surely if Blind Bull had hidden nearby and witnessed atrocities he would have related them to Bent. Did other Cheyennes who escaped and hid nearby see atrocities and pass the stories down in oral history? If so, why didn't Blind Bull hear these stories second- or thirdhand long before he gave his version to George Bent between 1914 and 1917? Previous to Powell's recording of the Cheyenne oral testimony of the elders in 1959, Mari Sandoz (1953), Platten (1959), and then other writers in later years writing from the Indian viewpoint compounded the atrocity story.

Thus, the oldest existing but not strictly original written documents even remotely corroborating Platten's claims, and the atrocity thesis in general, are white sources. Whether Cheyenne oral tradition drew from these white sources in later years is possible but cannot be proven. William D. Street, an early resident of Oberlin, Kansas, who visited the battle site shortly after the fight but was not himself present at the battle, claimed that "what was supposed to be a roll of plunder was carelessly tossed into a roaring fire of tepees and tepee poles, when an outcry told them that the roll contained a living human being, a little papoose."[46] The Street claim, published by the Kansas State Historical Society more than thirty years after the battle, is certainly the written genesis of the atrocity allegations, along with the claims of another early settler, F. M. Lockard, who published a similar story one year after Street.[47] Street claims his informant was one of the participant troopers, although he also alludes to the possibility that he may have received this "trooper's information third hand." Lockard claims as an informant "one of the buffalo hunters." Early in his narrative, Lockard refers to a hunter named James Rutledge as a source for much of his information, a person mentioned by no one else as having been present at Sappa Creek on April 23, 1875. This may have been thirdhand information. If Street's informant was Sergeant Platten or another soldier who witnessed Platten's alleged refusal to murder the woman and child, the story presented by Street in his article is certainly far different from Platten's version. Neither Street nor Lockard state when their informants related their tales. Neither does either man state why he waited more than thirty years to reveal this knowledge. As will be seen in Chapter VI, these factors are critical in evaluating Street's and Lockard's claims.

Even disregarding the amount of time between the battle and Lockard's account, as G. Derek West pointed out in 1968, Lockard's story is so hopelessly flawed with errors, even to the date and year of the battle, as to be suspect. As for Street's claim that a live infant was tossed into the burning tepees, he "makes no accusation of deliberate intent," West points out, "but attributes the deed to *carelessness*, a deed that may possibly have occurred."[48] Platten's claim that Henely ordered the murder would have been intentional, not "carelessness." West goes on to assert that Henely's men "can hardly be criticized for the methods employed in the destruction of the lodges, for this was the normal [army] procedure when an Indian camp was captured" in order to deprive the enemy of supplies necessary to continue fighting or fleeing. "Nor could Henely be blamed for his summary treatment of the dead," West continued. "There were probably no adequate tools for a conventional burial anyway, and to have tarried for any length of time on the Sappa could have endangered the safety of his command . . ."[49] Indeed, Lieutenant Henely states in his report that he felt "certain . . . other bands [of Indians] were in the vicinity [Spotted Wolf's party for certain] who would soon concentrate and attack me, and at least recapture the stock . . ."[50]

That burning lodges was common practice during the plains warfare of the 1870s there is no doubt. General Philip Sheridan officially recognized the practice's strategic importance and tactical practicality during the Washita campaign in 1868, and it was common through the Great Sioux War. That occasionally a still living but unconscious human being could have been burned mistakenly is not only possible but perhaps even probable. For sake of comparison, an early writer on the Indian campaigns, Captain R. G. Carter, a trusted subordinate to Colonel Ranald Mackenzie, asserts without consternation that during the 1873 raid of the 4th Cavalry into Mexico, Colonel Mackenzie's men burned an Indian village following an attack and that "wounded hostiles may have been killed in the burning lodges."[51]

Henely took no prisoners. A chance exists that one or more of the seriously wounded Indians were still alive but unconscious and appearing to be dead at the time the camp was burned. What is crucial is whether or not Henely or any of his men knew or suspected any of the victims to be still alive at the time of the burning. Did the command surgeon check the bodies? There is no indication in the reports that he did or did not. Such negligence, of course, would have been strictly against military policy and totally inexcusable by the codes of conduct of nineteenth-century warfare. The earliest testimony we have of such an alleged atrocity is that of Street, in 1908, who specifically asserts that the act was, at worst, "carelessness." If the burning of the live infant was blatantly intentional, surely someone would have leaked this information during the thirty-three years prior to 1908. And if it were unintentional carelessness, as Street claims, it pales in comparison with Platten's allegation that Lieutenant Henely specifically ordered him, in front of the other troopers, to murder a woman and her child.*

In any event, the importance of Street's claims lies not so much in the possible careless death of one Cheyenne noncombatant during the burning of the village as it does in what writers have made of both Street's and Lockard's accounts over the years. Beginning with Lockard's amazingly inaccurate recounting of the battle (he even had the year wrong) and continuing through a recent popular account of the fight by Andrew Hogarth and Kim Vaughan, the number of live Cheyenne cremations following the Battle of Sappa Creek has escalated. Claiming as a source one of the buffalo hunters, whom he would not identify, Lockard asserted there were a number of Cheyenne hiding in their lodges following the battle who were "dragged out, clubbed into insensibility and thrown into the fire."[52] Lockard infers here that because the Indians were clubbed *only* into "insensibility," Henely's men knew they were still alive at the time they were thrown into the fire. Undoubtedly, Street's and Lockard's claims were the source of the continued viewpoint so many writers—including Mari Sandoz, who like Lockard claimed the fight was largely between the Cheyennes and a large group of buffalo hunters and not the U.S. Army—have chosen to accept in order to draw more melodramatic conclusions.[53]

The magnificent prose, yet imagined dialogue, that flowed from the pen of the renowned Story Catcher of the Plains, Mari Sandoz, evoked powerful images of a massacre as "the smoke and smell of burning flesh spread

---

* Again, Platten's account is somewhat suspect on this point due to the date it was published (1959) by Thomas E. Way (after Platten's death) and to several major errors (of memory?) later in the narrative. The most glaring is Platten's recollection of killing the Cheyenne chief Whirlwind. Whirlwind was not at Sappa Creek. He was, at the time of the Red River War, an active peace chief trying to keep order among the Southern Cheyennes at Darlington Agency.

along the Sappa Fork," and "the hunters dug out more women and children, clubbed them, and threw them into the fire."[54] Sandoz ambiguously refers to papers of pioneers (Street and Lockard?) living on the plains in the late nineteenth century, along with old correspondence from personnel at Fort Wallace and recollections of "Old Cheyenne Woman and other Indians," whose anonymity Sandoz apparently wished to insure, as sources for her work. She also claims that whites in the Sappa Creek fight were composed mainly of civilian buffalo hunters, not soldiers. She tells how the Indians in the fight supposedly killed one hunter.[55] None of the other sources account for more than three buffalo hunters being in the fight.

Undoubtedly influenced by Sandoz's works, a regional Kansas writer, E. S. Sutton, wrote an article in 1961 based on the Street-Lockard accounts and added a number of historical errors of his own.[56]

As for picking up on Platten's account, Dan Thrapp in an article for Frontier Times in 1963 related Platten's story in total without comment or criticism of its possible self-glorifying embellishments and discernable factual errors.[57] In one of the more recent popular accounts of the 1990s, Andrew Hogarth and Kim Vaughan drew from Street and Lockard, expanding on their claims and writing that "the hunters proceeded to dig out and brutally murder those who had survived the three-hour fight. Henely ordered the village . . . to be burnt. A number [emphasis mine] of Cheyenne, including women and children were thrown into the fire while still alive."[58] None of the original accounts from participants at the Battle of Sappa Creek—including Platten, who openly accused Henely of ordering him to shoot a defenseless woman and child—assert that any noncombatant was burned alive, either intentionally or unintentionally. Neither does the main Cheyenne source, that of George Bent, even make mention of noncombatants murdered in any way by Henely's men after the fighting ceased. However, the reports of atrocities by Street and Lockard and advanced by Sandoz and others have, through the years, found their way into popular notions of the Sappa Creek fight.[59]

The questions remain. Did Henely and his men commit atrocities at Sappa Creek? Was the battle a massacre? Again, Henely took no prisoners.

Certainly it is conceivable that among all the "corpses" burned with the camp, one or more could have been alive and unconscious but appeared to be dead from severe wounds. Such negligence would not have been excused in 1875 but hardly constitutes willful intent. Father Peter John Powell has demonstrated in his work how, based on the old stories told to him by tribal elders in 1959, the atrocity-massacre thesis has become a part of Cheyenne oral tradition. Following the battle, "women slashed their legs with knives and the men caked their loosened hair with ashes and dust," Powell wrote. "Most terrible of all was the memory of the wounded women and children, tossed into the flames while they were still alive."[60] With the exception of George Bent, the work of Peter John Powell is the most fastidious from a strictly Cheyenne point of view. Unfortunately, white accounts of the Sappa Creek fight far outnumber the single contemporary Cheyenne account, of George Bent. This imbalance of evidence holds for most records of the Indian wars. Whites wrote their reminiscences—Indians did not. Most original Indian testimony is filtered through the eyes of white interpreters and ethnologists. Nevertheless, fairly accurate profiles of what *probably* happened may be reconstructed to fair degrees and include one to several logical and possible alternatives, all of which should be considered.[61] Future credible works of Indian history will need to acknowledge, at least as singular alternative explanations, the oral testimony handed down by Indian people. The question remains regarding Cheyenne oral testimony at Sappa Creek, however, that if Henely took no prisoners, were there Indians who escaped earlier and later returned and hid nearby and witnessed atrocities after the fighting ended? Logic dictates that any escapees would have left the scene for fear of detection and ridden as far away as possible, unless they had family members or close friends remaining in the camp and were thus concerned about their fate.

But what of those scholars who insist on the written documents as the only acceptable evidence? Based on the credible documents pertaining to Sappa Creek, the question continues to arise: How many noncombatants were murdered after the fighting ceased? Among the early secondary sources allegedly based on interviews of unnamed persons who participated in the fight, one according to Street, and an undisclosed number according to Lockard. Among the original sources, the only account that accused Henely of atrocities is Platten's, which blames Henely for ordering the murder of two Cheyenne noncombatants, a woman and a child, by shooting, not burning. Based on available credible sources, we can only conclude that an unknown number of wounded but unconscious Cheyenne people who appeared to be dead may have been carelessly burned in the destruction of Little Bull's village.

Was the Sappa Creek battle a massacre? Street claimed that Hill P. Wilson, the sutler at Fort Hays in 1875, asserted in 1905 that the army might have covered up the circumstances of the Sappa Creek affair. At the time, it was "understood," Wilson wrote in a letter to the Kansas State Historical Society, which Street included in his article, "that the least said about the affair the better for all concerned."[62] Recently, William Chalfant has raised the possibility that Henely reversed the Cheyenne casualty figures to account for more warriors being killed than women and children in order to avert the attention of eastern reformers and the press—an interesting possibility, considering that the army after the Sand Creek Massacre in 1864 went out of its way to try and avoid publicity regarding the deaths of women and children in the Indian wars.[63] Consider that young, ambitious junior officers on the military frontier after the Civil War found few command opportunities available in actual combat during any given year, a condition necessary for promotion. When opportunity presented itself, these officers wanted nothing in the official report that might cast a bad light on their command decisions in the field. Henely, at the time of the Sappa Creek fight, was supporting his mother financially. Perhaps his desire for promotion was even greater than most.

If we follow the dictionary definition of *massacre* as being the "indiscriminate" killing of people, particularly noncombatants, then we must declare Sappa Creek a massacre if we are to accept Street's and Lockard's claims. If we do not accept these claims, another important question presents itself. Did Little Bull's Cheyennes have a fair chance to surrender? According to Henely, Wheeler, and, perhaps surprisingly, Platten, they were offered surrender and refused before the fighting started. Robbins and Bent make no mention of any offer of surrender; both assert the Cheyenne camp was taken by surprise.

Certainly, if no offer of surrender was made by the 6th Cavalry, then a case could be made for massacre. Did the Cheyennes seek surrender after the fighting started, only to be shot down when attempting to parley, as many less than thorough secondary sources assert? No original white source admits to such action. Illumination on this issue comes, ironically, from the Indians. None other than Bent's informants (principally Blind Bull), who remain the closest available source we have from the Cheyennes that approaches original, place the blame for the frenzied shooting of Cheyenne defenders following the parley squarely on the shoulders of the warrior White Bear, for killing Sergeant Papier under a truce requested by the Indians themselves, an act considered treacherous by the cultural norms in 1875 of both whites and Cheyennes.

Similar to the scholars who have studied the Sappa Creek fight in the past, those who examine it in the future will probably never learn the exact truth regarding the number of deaths of noncombatants and the specific circumstances under which they died. Neither are we likely ever to completely resolve the accusations of atrocity and massacre in regard to numbers, methods, or whether or not persons were murdered after the fighting ceased. We may, however, learn much from the changing nature of the accusations themselves. As intriguing as the unknown details of the battle may continue to be, the differing interpretations of the Sappa Creek engagement have a wider significance. They can tell us much about American society's changing views of the Indian wars in American culture, an issue that will be explored in detail in the next chapter.

Notes

1. George Bent in Hyde, Life of George Bent, 368. The primary Cheyenne source for the Battle of Sappa Creek is George Bent in Hyde's account. Bent identifies his informants as Blind Bull and Spotted Wolf, the Southern Cheyenne. Although Spotted Wolf was not in the camp, he was good friends with Little Bull; thus, he possessed a special interest in ascertaining the details of the fight from those who escaped, especially if his friends were killed. See Powell, People of the Sacred Mountain, 2:1357 n. 7.

2. Henely's Report, 91.

3. Ibid., 90; George Bent in Hyde, *Life of George Bent*, 368; Wheeler, *Buffalo Days*, 105. The man who visited the battlefield the most, William D. Street, compiled the most complete description of the site, although it contains slight errors regarding troop positions, complete with a map sketch. See Street, "Cheyenne Indian Massacre," 369–371.

4. Henely's Report, 90.

5. Wheeler, *Buffalo Days*, 104–105.

6. Henely's Report, 90.

7. Whceler, *Buffalo Days*, 105; Platten's Account, 11; Henely's Report, 90.

8. Platten's Account, 11.

9. Robbins's Account, 198.

10. Wheeler, *Buffalo Days*, 105.

11. Henely's Report, 90.

12. George Bent in Hyde, *Life of George Bent*, 368.

13. Platten's Account, 11.

14. Wheeler, *Buffalo Days*, 105.

15. Robbins's Account, 199.

16. Henely's Report, 90.

17. Platten's Account, 11.

18. Wheeler, *Buffalo Days*, 105.

19. Kansas State Historical Society, "The Last of the Rank and File Whose Blood Drenched Kansas Soil," *Collections of the Kansas State Historical Society,* 12 (1911–1912): xvii.

20. George Bent in Hyde, *Life of George Bent*, 368.

21. Henely's Report, 90.

22. Ibid.

23. Henely's Report, 90.

24. Robbins's Account, 199.

25. Kansas State Historical Society, "The Last of the Rank and File," xvii.

26. Platten's Account, 11.

27. Wheeler, *Buffalo Days*, 105.

28. Robbins's Account, 199.

29. Wheeler, *Buffalo Days*, 106.

30. Henely's Report, 90.

31. George Bent in Hyde, *Life of George Bent*, 368.

32. Henely's Report, 90.

33. Ibid.

34. Wheeler, *Buffalo Days*, 106.

35. Platten's Account, 11.

36. George Bent in Hyde, *Life of George Bent*, 368–369.

37. Platten's Account, 11.

38. Robbins's Account, 199.

39. Henely's Report, 90.

40. See Street, "Cheyenne Indian Massacre," 371. One other early settler, August C. Blume, claimed to be near the battle site at the time of the fight. Blume claimed he could hear the firing from some distance away. See Bernice Larson Webb, "First Homesteader and the Battle of Sappa Creek," *Kansas Quarterly* 10, no. 3 (summer 1978): 52–58.

41. Ibid.

42. George Bent in Hyde, *Life of George Bent*, 368–369. See also Powell, *People of the Sacred Mountain*, 2:904.

43. Henely's Report, 91.

44. Platten's Account, 12.

45. Powell, *People of the Sacred Mountain*, 2:1357 n. 10.

46. Street, "Cheyenne Indian Massacre," 372.

47. See Lockard, "The Battle of Achilles."

48. West, "The Battle of Sappa Creek," 175.

49. Ibid., 177.

50. Henely's Report, 91.

51. See R. G. Carter, *On the Border With Mackenzie or Winning West Texas from the Comanches* (New York: Antiquarian Press, Ltd., 1961), 439ff; West, "The Battle of Sappa Creek," 177 n. 71.

52. Lockard, "The Battle of Achilles," 29.

53. See West, "The Battle of Sappa Creek," 174–178.

54. Sandoz, *Cheyenne Autumn*, 123.

55. Ibid., 328.

56. E. S. Sutton, "Sappa—Meaning Black Hope—April 25, 1875, in Indian Battles in Rawlins County," Rawlins County, Kansas Historical Society (1961) 3–10.

57. Thrapp, "Attack on Sappa Creek," 40, 68–69. It would be verbose and result in unproductive and cumbersome redundancy to tally all the factual Street-Lockard-Sandoz errors, such as dates and the names of participants who were not at Sappa Creek, that found their way into most of these later popular accounts. For some of these errors, see Chalfant, *Cheyennes at Dark Water Creek*, 147–159, 166–169.

58. Andrew Hogarth and Kim Vaughn, *Battlefields, Monuments and Markers: A Guide to Native American & United States Army Engagements from 1854–1890* (Sydney: Andrew Hogarth Publishing, 1993), 40. See also Andrew Hogarth and Kim Vaughn, *Cheyenne Hole* (Oberlin, Kans.: Last Indian Raid Museum, 1991), 1–24.

59. See West, "The Battle of Sappa Creek," for the earliest detailed discrediting of many of these accounts. West compares their assertions to the specific details reported in all original sources, with the exception of Bent.

60. Powell, *People of the Sacred Mountain*, 2:904.

61. See Margot Liberty, "Oral and Written Indian Perspectives on the Indian Wars," in *Legacy: New Perspectives on the Battle of the Little Bighorn*, ed. Charles E. Rankin (Helena: Montana Historical Society Press, 1996), 125–138.

62. Street, "Cheyenne Indian Massacre," 369 n. 1.

63. Chalfant, *Cheyennes at Dark Water Creek*, 158–159.

Chapter VI

The Sappa Creek Massacre:
Commentary and Conclusions

The thrifty farmers who raise alfalfa on this same ground today little
suspect the thrilling scenes enacted there thirty-five years ago.

—F. M. Lockard, 1909

Following the burning of Little Bull's camp, at about noon on April
23, 1875, H Company, 6th Cavalry began their return to Fort Wallace. The
bodies of Sergeant Papier and Private Theims were carried in a wagon
along with eight captured Cheyenne rifles. The command also drove a
herd of 134 captured horses.[1] With the troops were a number of souve-
nirs Henely and some of his men had picked up from the battlefield.
Several of these items later became the cause of controversy and intrigue.

"There was found in the camp of the Indians a memorandum-book
containing rude though expressive sketches, made by themselves, of their
exploits," Henely reported. "Among a great number were the following, as
I interpret them: The charge on the scouts at the battle of Red River; the
attack on Adobe Walls and on Major [Wyllys] Lyman's wagon train; the
killing of private [James H.] Pettyjohn,* and another (of which I am not
certain) representing the murder of the German family."[2]

———

* Private James H. Pettyjohn, Company M, 6th Cavalry, was killed earlier on McClellan Creek in
Texas. Henely's men claimed that one of the horses captured at Sappa Creek, branded "M," had
belonged to Private Pettyjohn.

The men took several war bonnets as trophies when the camp was plundered. Homer Wheeler took one from the warrior he claimed was the last killed in the final assault, possibly White Bear. Later Wheeler presented the war bonnet to "General Pope at Fort Leavenworth, Kansas, after coming into the army." Wheeler noted that war bonnets would "readily bring in trade one or two ponies . . ."[3] Henely stated that one of the war bonnets was surmounted by two horns. Although Henely ignorantly surmised this signified high position, that of a "medicine man," such horned bonnets were not uncommon among the Cheyennes.[4] Sergeant Frederick Platten also claimed to have taken a war bonnet from the Indian he erroneously identified as the council chief Whirlwind. "I returned to where the dead chief lay on the ground," Platten asserted, "and took his war bonnet, a thing of rare beauty trimmed with lots of elk teeth and many colored beads. Lieutenant Hanley [sic] and Captain [Adna R.] Chaffee later took this war bonnet to New York, to show it to some friends. They promised faithfully that they would return it. However, I never saw the bonnet again and do not know what became of it."[5] Private Marcus M. Robbins merely noted that the camp was "rich in buffalo robes, beaded moccasins, war bonnets and the different adornments of savage life . . ."[6] Bent's informants claim Henely took White Bear's war bonnet, "tipped with two buffalo horns," as well as a silver belt from the corpse of Yellow Body Woman.[7]

A forced march of about thirty-eight miles brought the command to Monument Station on the old Smoky Hill Road to Denver by the morning of April 24. Later the same day the command made its way to the site of Sheridan Station, where the men bivouacked. But that night H Company was overtaken by one of the famous "northers" that can hit the Great Plains in April. Henely's men found themselves in the midst of a blizzard producing nearly two feet of snow. "After a night of intense suffering among horses and men," Henely remembered, "the men having but one blanket each, and no tents—some of the men being frozen, and others who had dug holes in the bank for shelter, requiring to be dug out of the snow by their comrades—the storm abated and we split up in small squads to search for the captured stock [which had wandered away during the storm]."[8]

Homer Wheeler reveals how he and Lieutenant C. C. Hewitt found shelter in an "old section house" during the night.[9] The morning sun revealed an endless blanket of white. "We tried to rustle wood to build fires with, but found none," Sergeant Platten remembered. "We finally had to use bacon for fuel."[10] Soon the men noticed that several of their comrades were missing. "Doctor Atkins suggested that the [missing] men might be covered with snow," Wheeler remembered. "He found a pole and commenced to poke it into some of the drifts where he thought they might be. Finally, he heard a faint cry," Wheeler continued, " 'Stop that! You are hurting me; get off my feet!' " Several men immediately dug out their comrades from under a small bank in a protected pocket, where they had slept, as Wheeler put it, "like a bug in a rug."[11]

The men took most of the day to round up missing livestock. Their task was difficult because, as Platten remembered, "the glare on the snow was blinding; not a few of our soldiers were snow blinded." Many of the captured Indian ponies were not recovered.* [12] Although sunburned and snow-blind, the command soon made its way back to Fort Wallace, where "nearly all of us," Private Marcus M. Robbins recalled, went "on sick report . . ."[13] Within about two weeks, during which time Lieutenant Henely wrote his official report commending his men and received praise for his actions from post commander Major Hambright and department commander General Pope, Company H, 6th Cavalry made its way back by rail to its post at Fort Lyon, Colorado Territory. At Fort Lyon the company's comrades in the 19th Infantry gave them "a royal welcome," Private Robbins remembered, "the band and all the garrison turning out to receive us."[14]

In the spring of 1876 the army ordered Lieutenant Austin Henely and the 6th Cavalry to Arizona Territory, where they relieved elements of the 5th

---

* According to Henely's Report, about ninety horses were recovered. After the command returned to Fort Wallace, some of Homer Wheeler's employees rounded up many of the missing Indian ponies. Later Wheeler was told he had to turn them over to the army. He cut out several, apparently without anyone knowing. See Wheeler, *Buffalo Days*, 110. The remaining captured stock were sold at auction. Department commander General John Pope proposed that the proceeds, amounting to about $1,000, be used for the benefit of the German sisters, but bureaucratic red tape prevented this. See West, "The Battle of Sappa Creek," 165.

Cavalry at Fort Bowie in Apache Pass, along the line of the old Butterfield Mail route through Cochise County. Henely carried with him a prophecy of his own death, the first of many events that would enhance the intrigue surrounding the Sappa Creek fight. In a letter dated August 17, 1905, by Hill P. Wilson, a former post trader at Fort Hays, to the Kansas State Historical Society and related by Street in 1908, Lieutenant Henely had among his effects at Fort Lyon, before the 6th Cavalry departed for Arizona, one of the war bonnets taken at Sappa Creek.

One day at Fort Lyon the Cheyenne wife of Arkansas Valley cattle baron John Prowers, Amache, "Walking Woman," daughter of Lone Bear (One Eye), saw the war bonnet and recognized it as belonging to an important member of her people. According to Wilson, when Amache Prowers saw Henely's trophy "she 'took on,' " as Wilson put it, "and went through the mourning ceremonies of the tribe. She kept up the crooning and wailing for three days and nights." When her mourning ended, "she refreshed herself and made a prediction that 'the man who is responsible for the death of [one whom Wilson, out of ignorance, referred to as a medicine man] will die within a year.' "[15] Although George Bent claimed the war bonnet in question was the horned one taken from the body of White Bear at Sappa Creek, Mari Sandoz in the 1950s asserted that the war bonnet belonged to Medicine Arrows, the keeper of Maahotse.

Cheyenne historian Father Peter John Powell has discredited Sandoz's claim by establishing that Medicine Arrows had, during the winter of 1874–1875, prior to the Sappa Creek fight, safely made his way north across the Kansas escape corridor to safety among the Northern Cheyennes. He died peacefully in the north, perhaps in the Powder River country, in 1876.[16] Medicine Arrow's son, Black Hairy Dog, however, escaped the embattled camp at Sappa Creek with his wife. White Bear was the stepson of Black Hairy Dog. Powell surmises that the war bonnet could have been loaned or entrusted to Black Hairy Dog, not an uncommon practice, to protect his stepson in battle. Perhaps White Bear was even wearing the bonnet when he was killed at Sappa Creek.

Because Amache Prowers had no way of knowing that Medicine Arrows was not at Sappa Creek, she probably assumed his presence at Little Bull's camp and thus mourned his death. This theory could account for both Bent's and Sandoz's claims,[17] although Sandoz elected to fictionalize her version of the Sappa Creek story further by asserting that Medicine Arrows was buried after Sappa Creek (not burned like all the other victims). Sandoz asserted Medicine Arrows was shot down under a flag of truce during the battle.[18]

Undoubtedly, Lieutenant Henely departed Fort Lyon for Arizona Territory, despite Amache's prediction of his demise, content in the belief that he and his men had advanced the cause of the republic at the conclusion of the Red River War. Had he lived a long life, he probably would not have completely understood the far-reaching extent of the accusations later made against him, beginning more than thirty years after the Battle of Sappa Creek, by the civilians Street and Lockard, accusations that constitute popular perception to the present day. It's doubtful that Henely would have grasped the symbolic power of the accusations in relation to the times in which he lived and to the sweeping events in which he played a minor role. For the symbolism surrounding the speculation of what may or may not have taken place at Little Bull's doomed camp on April 23, 1875, transcends the importance of conclusively knowing what actions were committed and what actions were not.

The Sappa Creek "Massacre" is a vivid but singular example that can illuminate Americans' changing perceptions of the Indian Wars and the theme of western conquest in the nineteenth century and since as it was played out on the windswept plains of Kansas. Like the mysteries surrounding the specific events of the engagement, these long-range interpretations, although ultimately speculative, nevertheless reflect changing attitudes and worldviews. This evolving body of thought suggests certain possibilities that, unlike more scientific dogma, is the essence of dynamic history. We must be mindful that the first public claims of atrocity and massacre at Sappa Creek occurred during the first decade of the twentieth century, more than thirty years after the battle. Why not earlier?

Between 1875, when the Sappa Creek battle was fought, and 1900, an era Mark Twain dubbed the Gilded Age, few Americans other than the Indians themselves challenged the determination of Euro-American civilization to possess the Great Plains. This was a time when the overwhelming majority of white Americans placed unrelenting faith in the goodness of capitalism, Christianity, and expanding industrialism. Only a few socialists and anarchists challenged the triumphant celebration of American achievement. But these intellectuals and disgruntled workers were viewed as weird eccentrics. Like the Indians, they were seen as unfit to control resource-rich land because of their rejection of the basic Puritan tenets of individualism, thrift, and industry as prescribed by a laissez-faire federal government and the unrestricted world market.

Men like Austin Henely, his superiors, and his subordinates, saw themselves doing good things as agents of this empire. So did the general public, who read of these men's exploits in the many newspapers of the pervasively jingoist press of the era. Indeed, the continental imperialism that characterized the conquest of the U.S. frontier was seen as one small segment of a largely global imperialism that brought Europeans new lands, labor, and natural resources from America to Africa to Asia. Toward the end of the era, in 1898, the United States entered the global imperialistic arena by ousting Spain from its last tenuous footholds in the western hemisphere and Asia. Driven by the theory of social Darwinism and the "white man's burden," the colonialism and conquest that marked this age was viewed as a kind of natural selection resulting in a logical and orderly stratification of mankind based on race and class. During this age it was fashionable to view the conquest of the American West as a struggle between savagery and civilization, a notion that persisted deep into the twentieth century.

So the "savage" nature of the West and its earliest inhabitants was merely a small part of worldwide savagery that awaited redemption by Europeans. In many ways the rural based populism that swept the Great Plains during the last decade of the century like a prairie fire reinforced rather than challenged this concept by attempting to reempower the rural middle class and their "pioneer" virtues. Within such a social environment, Indian cultures had little chance with either the agrarians or the industrialists. They had at first been viewed as dependent nations. Later they were viewed as racial inferiors whose future depended on assimilation into the lower strata of the natural social system, a system made worse by failed legislation designed to break up tribal cohesion, such as the Dawes Severalty Act of 1887. Certainly Indian "tribes" had no divinely ordered rights to possess resource-rich lands that were needed to fuel the engine of modern progress. If the agent of empire, the U.S. Army, behaved brutally in abstract places like the valley of Sappa Creek, few Americans would question the validity of its actions when compared to such savage assaults on Christianity, gentility, and civilization as the massacre of the John German family. Subordinating Indians became synonymous with subordinating lower classes of all kinds, both domestic and foreign.[19]

Most non-Indians in the West felt that the future of their communities, as well as of their livelihoods, depended on Indian "removal" and assimilation. The perception of Indian peoples held by the settlers who lived in their midst was vastly different from the perceptions held by many eastern reformers whose families had not invaded Indian lands in recent generations and who lived far from consequential danger. Few western settlers would raise a voice against questionable military actions against the Indians when the source of their fears too frequently was the perceived lack of a sufficient military presence to protect them.[20]

But Americans' attitudes began changing in subtle ways with the new century and the passing of Indian independence. Unlike the populism of the 1890s, the social reforms that emerged between 1900 and World War I occurred during a time of general prosperity. A new middle-class awareness among urban dwellers challenged monopoly and called for a broadening of the population's power base. Although so-called progressivism did not advocate racial equality, a new awareness of vanquished primitive cultures became a sentimental reality for many affluent Americans. A preoccupation with the perceived wholesome values of the closed and hence idealized "frontier" was integrated into the social fabric of America. In a sense, this nostalgia, symbolized by the popular image of the nation's president and former Dakota rancher, Theodore Roosevelt, challenged, although passively, some of the tenets of the Indian reform movement, particularly total assimilation, while still recognizing a certain justifiable inevitability. For a few, there was a return to a belief in the virtues of Rousseau's noble savage.[21] Some lamented, although hypocritically, the lost "color" of ancient societies alongside their self-praise of modern progress and a rekindled interest in the reminiscences of the old soldiers.

Although Helen Hunt Jackson put forward arguments for Indian rights in *A Century of Dishonor* in 1881, her pleas made little impression on the thinking of most middle-class Americans until the turn of the century. For many easterners, and for more than a few westerners who remembered the old West—now that their lands and lives were safe from Indians—tribal ways became a subject of fascination. Like James R. Mead, who mourned the passing of the buffalo after he had participated in the herds' wholesale slaughter, many of those who had fought or lived among Indians nostalgically lamented the Indians' passing.[22] For some, injustices against Indians were considered for the first time, only because any danger posed by Indians was a thing of the past. An argument can be made that William D. Street and F. M. Lockard, the Rawlins County settlers who first suggested that Sappa Creek was a massacre, were influenced by these changing social perceptions. As time passed and the land and its people changed, so did Street's and Lockard's views of the Cheyennes. Such changes are reflected in their writing.

Both Street and Lockard wrote their versions of the Sappa Creek fight (1908 and 1909, respectively) during an epochal decade in the United States. Progressivism was at its zenith. Kansas had been settled, the Indians removed, and the prairie states in general enjoyed a booming world agricultural market. There were many original settlers still alive whose stories were in demand as testimony to those who conquered the land. Often, judging from their reminiscences, many of these were men and women who, within the comfortable bounds of their collective security, viewed aspects of the frontier with a nostalgic eye. In some of their reminiscences can be detected arrogance toward those who came to the land after them, and sometimes a self-righteous nostalgia for the passing of former frontier residents, especially Indians. As F. M. Lockard, for a time a district court judge in western Kansas, wrote in his article on Sappa Creek for *Kansas Magazine* in 1909: "The thrifty farmers who raise alfalfa on this same ground today little suspect the thrilling scenes enacted there thirty-five years ago."[23]

The progressive slant both Street and Lockard gave to their versions of the Sappa Creek story are only meaningful when compared directly with their almost unknown writings regarding Cheyenne-white conflict, which each wrote a decade or more before their Sappa Creek articles appeared in print. During the autumn of 1878 a few members of Little Wolf's and Dull Knife's contingent of Northern Cheyennes fled north to seek refuge among the Lakotas after their complaints about being prevented from returning from their displacement on the Southern Cheyenne reservation in Indian Territory fell on the U.S. government's deaf ears. Along the way a few of the warriors, despite the chiefs' pleas to refrain from making war on civilians, killed between seventeen and forty white settlers along Sappa Creek and Beaver Creek in northwest Kansas.

Often the Northern Cheyennes were pressured by troops and fought them on their way north through the state. Many writers since that time, including George Bent, ascribed the killings of settlers in Kansas to the brutal but customary tradition of revenge, strong among the Plains tribes, and in this case taken for the killing of Little Bull's people at Sappa Creek. Some writers made these claims even though Little Bull's party were southerners and Dull Knife's party were northerners and tension existed between the two groups on the Indian Territory reservation in 1878. Views concerning whether the Little Wolf–Dull Knife raids were revenge for Sappa Creek have been debated over the years. Some of those supporting the revenge-motive theory attempt to maintain empathy for the plight of the northerners by trying to justify the killings as a fair response to Henely's actions. Others attempt to dispel empathy by painting a picture of Cheyenne savagery.[24] Other analysts, especially Kansas historian Ramon Powers, have challenged the revenge motive altogether.

The earliest reputable published account linking the Sappa Creek fight and the Dull Knife raids by the revenge theory is William D. Street's 1908 article on the Sappa Creek battle, written for the Kansas State Historical Society. "On September 30 and Oct 1, 1878," Street wrote,

> a band of Northern Cheyennes, under the leadership of Chief Dull Knife—surged eastward—and wreaked fearful revenge on the innocent white people who had pushed their settlements out onto the Sappa and Beaver Creeks—nearly forty unsuspecting men were killed, women outraged, and a vast amount of property destroyed—The massacre of the Cheyennes

by Lieutenant Henely and the massacre of the white settlers by Dull Knife's
band of [Northern] Cheyennes, always appeared to me to be closely connected in the annals of border warfare, now a closed book forever.[25]

Whether or not Street, when he wrote this passage, sympathized with
the plight of Little Wolf's and Dull Knife's northerners, as he clearly did
with Little Bull's southerners, thus purposefully establishing the revenge
explanation, is unclear. What is clear, however, is that in 1878, when Little
Wolf's and Dull Knife's people swept through Kansas, William D. Street was
quite eager to get rid of them, regardless whether or not vengeance for the
earlier Sappa Creek fight was justifiable.

In 1878, William D. Street was a rancher in northwest Kansas. During
the Little Wolf–Dull Knife exodus, Street was employed by Captain Clarence
Mauck, 4th Cavalry, to carry dispatches from the Holstine Ranch near Atwood,
Kansas, to Ogallala, Nebraska, a distance of over 135 miles.[26] Street kept
detailed notes of his adventure and later donated the original unpublished
manuscript to the Kansas State Historical Society, where it remains today.
Prior to his employment with the army, Street rode into the ranch of Samuel
Holstine determined to "hunt down the Indians." At the ranch, Holstine
formed a posse that included William D. Street. " 'The Indians have killed
every man for miles, below here and over on the Sappa,' " Street wrote of
Holstine's conversation with him that day. " 'And we are making up a crowd
to follow them up, and help the troops kill or capture them; we want you to
go along.' I told him I was ready to go," Street said, although his horse was
worn out. Holstine then instructed one of his ranch hands to "catch that big
fat sorrel horse for Bill Street, he is going with us."[27]

Although undated, Street's manuscript was most likely written much
earlier than his article about the Sappa Creek fight. Nowhere in the manuscript does he make any reference to a revenge motive connecting the Dull
Knife killings on the Sappa and Henely's fight in 1875, a connection he
does make in the 1908 article. This is an important piece of logic he surely
would not have left out of the Dull Knife manuscript had he written that
manuscript after the Sappa Creek article. Indeed, Street's rhetoric in the earlier manuscript concerns his fear for the safety of livestock owned by his

friends and neighbors in northwest Kansas. Nowhere in the early manuscript does he show the sympathy for the Cheyennes that he would later demonstrate in the 1908 article about the Sappa Creek Massacre.

In 1894, the Honorable F. M. Lockard published a now-obscure book with the Champion Press of Norton, Kansas, titled *The History of the Early Settlement of Norton County, Kansas*. The price was fifty cents. The book rather loosely details more than information about Norton County. Lockard, who apparently had no direct involvement in the Little Wolf–Dull Knife exodus of 1878–1879, nevertheless vividly describes the Dull Knife attacks in the Sappa Creek and Beaver Creek valleys. His words are filtered through the reminiscence of a friend he interviewed for the purpose, a cowboy named Gus Cook, who *was* on the scene in 1878. Cook recalled, for example, how he arrived at a homestead in the Sappa Creek valley on October 2. "There lay the husband and father," Lockard quoted Cook, "and outside the door was the wife and children. The eldest girl had a bed quilt around her for a dress . . . This sight," Cook emphasized, "would have cured those who pity the poor Indian."[28]

Although Lockard, like Street, made the revenge connection between the Dull Knife raids and the Sappa Creek Massacre in his 1909 article on the Sappa Creek fight for *Kansas Magazine*, his earlier 1894 book makes no mention of the Sappa Creek Massacre. Lockard states in his 1909 article that one of the Sappa Creek buffalo hunters informed him that the burning of surviving Cheyennes in Little Bull's camp following the fight "was the most cruel and heart rending scene he had ever witnessed, that when the smell of burning flesh reached him, he turned aside and went to camp."[29] Surely if Lockard had been given this story prior to 1894, when he published his book, he would have included the account of the 1875 Sappa Creek Massacre, at the very least attributing the Little Wolf–Dull Knife attacks so vividly depicted by Gus Cook to revenge for Henely's actions in 1875.

Assuming for a moment that Lockard was indeed told of atrocities at Sappa Creek by one of the buffalo hunters after 1894, why had it taken this informant nearly twenty years or more after the battle to relate the tale to someone who would write about it? Had this "buffalo hunter" been employed in some contract capacity by the military, therefore fearing punishment for telling the tale? Surely any such business relationship would have ended long before 1894. Could it be that the buffalo hunter waited until the early 1900s to tell the story, or could Lockard have been told the tale earlier and simply waited until 1909 to reveal it? If so, why the delays?

Could it be that attitudes governing Indian humanity were perceived differently in the minds of whites like F. M. Lockard and his anonymous buffalo hunter between 1875 and 1900, when final conquest was being celebrated, than they were in 1909 during the wake of the Progressive era, when Lockard published his massacre-oriented story on the Sappa Creek fight? Or could it be that Lockard was simply not to be upstaged by a rival pioneer author, W. D. Street, who published his account a year earlier? In his 1909 article, Lockard also blasts a 1906 article, loosely based on Sappa Creek by Will Kenyon, as being inaccurate because it said nothing of a massacre or atrocities.[30] Then Lockard incorporates much of Kenyon's inaccuracies into his own article.* Perhaps Lockard simply embellished Kenyon's earlier (erroneous) information while playing up Street's original atrocity theme. If this was the case, Lockard did a poor job, not even citing the year of the battle correctly.†

We may of course only surmise possibilities, because Street and Lockard are long gone. But we may conclude with certainty that the writing of both men regarding the Indian-white conflict in Kansas during the 1870s changed dramatically over time in both attitude and tone, reflecting changes in perceptions and values. In their later writings (1908 and 1909), composed during the Progressive era, both men are sympathetic to Indians. In their earlier writings, both men are unsympathetic to Indians.

By the 1920s, in the wake of a return to normalcy and isolationism following the Great War, American attitudes shifted again. Despite the popu-

---

* Both Lockard in 1909 and Kenyon 1906, for example, make the unfounded claim that the Suhtai camp on Sappa Creek was led by the warrior Spotted Horse.

† Robbins's account in *Deeds of Valor* is an exception to the Progressive era trend of scrutinizing the Sappa Creek massacre by humanizing the Indian and suggesting atrocities were committed. Many veteran soldiers, however, said little or nothing about the humanity of Indians until long after the fight, if ever.

lar images of bathtub gin and the liberated flapper, the 1920s and to some extent the following three decades, were a time of return to what the popular press called 100 percent Americanism. Translated into action at the grassroots, 100 percent Americanism meant intolerance of things foreign and nonwhite. The twenties witnessed a revival of the Ku Klux Klan and a growth in overt and covert racism to epic proportions. The decade was also marked by a resurgence of religious fundamentalism. Native Americans did not fit the white definition of 100 percent Americanism.

The earlier nostalgia for lost Indian customs gave way among many persons still enchanted with the old frontier to patriotic reverence for the stories of old, lesser known, veteran soldiers. From Britton Davis to Anton Mazzonovich to Homer Wheeler, these stories were told. Some veterans, notably Britton Davis, were somewhat sympathetic to their former Indian enemies. Homer Wheeler, who accepted a commission in the 5th Cavalry in 1875, following the Sappa Creek fight, published his memoirs first in 1923 as The Frontier Trail, and again in 1925 as Buffalo Days. His writing, although somewhat paternalistic, reflected the times in which it was written. As did Britton Davis and others, Wheeler clearly recognizes the humanity of the Indians he fought and acknowledges injustices committed against them. This point of view challenged some notions prevalent in the 1920s that originally fueled the demand for the soldiers' stories.

But while retaining a bit of romantic nostalgia for the Indians, Wheeler does not apologize for the invasion of Indian lands, regarding it as a logical sequence in an age-old process of conquest. Neither does he cast aspersions on the actions of Lieutenant Austin Henely or any of his command at the Sappa Creek fight. To the contrary, he highly praises both officers and enlisted men. Although he admits that Little Bull's village was "wiped out," as he put it, he obviously perceived no unacceptable behavior in the manner in which the Indians were wiped out.[31] Wheeler's Buffalo Days remains the most nonjudgmental account of the fight written in the twentieth century. But the perceived inevitability and justice of white conquest remains intact in the tone of Wheeler's writing at the same time he praises the bravery and determination of the losers, after they were no longer a threat to Euro-American civilization. One wonders if Wheeler could have conveyed his attitudes more expressively had he illustrated his book with one of the era's famous photographs, depicting President Calvin Coolidge wearing a three-piece suit and a resplendent war bonnet.

Despite the nostalgic counterbalance felt by those who embraced the "lost civilization" point of view of the early twentieth century, it was during the forty-year period between 1920 and 1960 that the western myth, first spawned by Frederick Jackson Turner in 1893, gained popularity in relation to the Far West. During that time the old genre western of dime-novel fame made its way to Hollywood, and the myth of the white conquest of the old frontier came into its own. In the wake of these patriotic perceptions of the West, only a few brave writers dared to challenge prevailing wisdom. Arguably the most important of these rebels was Mari Sandoz. Her version of the Sappa Creek Massacre and the idea that Indian revenge connected it and the Little Wolf–Dull Knife exodus of 1878–1879 were undoubtedly influenced by Street and Lockard (certainly not by George Bent), because she mentions the Street and Lockard accounts in her rough notes for *Cheyenne Autumn*.[32] Her fictionalized efforts to establish the Sappa Creek fight as a true massacre, in which atrocities were committed, gained steam during the Vietnam era of the 1960s and 1970s, the time of the awakening Red Power movement. Her views persist to the present day.

The best-seller *Cheyenne Autumn* appeared in 1953. Sergeant Frederick Platten's account accusing Henely of ordering the execution of a Cheyenne woman and her child appeared in 1959. Could Sandoz have influenced Platten, or was he telling the truth? If his account is accurate, why did he not make it known much earlier, say during the first decade of the twentieth century, as a complement to Street's and Lockard's accusations? He had nothing to fear at that time from his old commander, for Lieutenant Austin Henely was long dead. Living in Arizona, however, Platten may have been unaware of Street's and Lockard's articles published in Kansas journals. In any event, the timing of his accusations calls them into question. Nevertheless, Platten and Sandoz would influence popular perception of the Sappa Creek Massacre during the 1960s and 1970s.

Finally, at a time of sweeping change in societal attitudes among some of the nation's youth during the 1960s and 1970s, and in the wake of the Civil Rights movement, many credible studies of Indian historical perspectives were published for an appreciative audience. In 1966 the Bent-Hyde manuscript, complete with the Cheyenne account of the Sappa Creek fight, turned up in an attic and was published two years later.[33] George B. Grinnell's work, The Fighting Cheyennes, first published in 1915, reappeared three years after Cheyenne Autumn, in 1956, republished by the University of Oklahoma Press. It was published several times more during the 1960s and later. Grinnell's older works, The Cheyenne Indians and By Cheyenne Campfires, reappeared during the 1960s. In 1960, E. Adamson Hoebel's classic ethnology The Cheyennes: Indians of the Great Plains was published. In 1963 Donald Berthrong's fine study The Southern Cheyennes was published, and Yale University Press brought out John Stands In Timber and Margot Liberty's Cheyenne Memories in 1967. In 1969 the University of Oklahoma Press published Peter John Powell's two-volume Sweet Medicine: The Continuing Role of the Sacred Arrows, the Sun Dance, and the Sacred Buffalo Hat in Northern Cheyenne History.

Between 1960 and 1970 less-scholarly works about the Indian wars appeared. Dee Brown's Bury My Heart at Wounded Knee: An Indian History of the American West, 1970, an overview that included the Cheyennes, became both a national best-seller as well as the source of controversy among critics. Arguably this book, although lacking sound historical methodology, became a catalyst for the modern revisionist movement in western history. Surprisingly, Brown's capsulated coverage of the Red River War of 1875 makes no mention of the Sappa Creek Massacre.

Certainly the most absurd secondary account of the Sappa Creek fight written to date was the article by Gene Jones for Real West in 1963. His point of view was not so much sympathetic toward Indians as it was reflective of the era's budding discontent with the U.S. military presence in questionable places and situations. Using manufactured dialogue, Jones portrayed Henely as a psychotic killer who

> From the moment of the attack at dawn, . . . Henely pushed his men relentlessly, bellowing hoarsely over the crackle of the rifle fire.
> "Fire! Keep firing!" he ordered. "Keep shooting till every dirty redskin in that camp is dead!"

Henely's body trembled with excitement. His sweating, unshaven face was a devil-mask of hatred, and his speech became thick, as if he were drunk. Again and again he shouted the order to fire, in a kind of hypnotic chant . . . [Then] Lieutenant Henely ran into the Cheyenne camp, shooting at a body here and there that he thought might still be alive . . . At the entrance to one of the tepees a papoose lay whimpering on its dead mother's body, Henely kicked the body inside, tossed the baby in after it, and set fire to the tepees.[34]

The last sentence is obviously a spin on Street and Lockard and perhaps even Platten's account, published only four years before Jones's story.

In the vanguard of the twenty-first century, an age of cultural hypersensitivity created in part by a resurgence of conservative values that challenge some entrenched premises of cultural relativism, many of the claims regarding the Sappa Creek fight advanced by Street, Lockard, and Platten remain politically correct to both the public and academia. The massacre-atrocity thesis persists despite efforts over the years by historians like G. Derek West to point out the lack of original source support for such a thesis. The discovery and availability of the Bent-Hyde material in 1968 gives us the earliest written Cheyenne version of the fight (it was originally written prior to 1918, when Bent died), and although it does not support the atrocity thesis, it does suggest that more women and children were killed than warriors. Bent's account does not alter popular perceptions, however, regarding living persons being burned alive after the fight. Father Peter John Powell's *People of the Sacred Mountain*, which utilizes the Bent-Hyde material, nevertheless supports the massacre-atrocity thesis based on Street, Lockard, and Cheyenne oral testimony.

As exemplified by West's arguments, there currently exists at the turn of the twenty-first century a budding "realist" school of thought that seeks understanding through an exact accounting of facts as they pertain to specific events. Although all history is to some degree political, realists reject broad interpretations based on current values and worldviews that are designed to challenge historical cultural assumptions—a forceful agenda-driven methodology that realists and others term "presentism," a kind of intragenerational ethnocentrism. Historians and the public alike often find themselves polarized more than in any previous era over divergence in thinking pertaining to controversial and sensitive topics like the Indian wars.

Such differences in logic would probably be lost on men like Medicine Water and Lieutenant Austin Henely, who, from the point of view of the realist, were in significant ways as much alike as they were different. Both men came from cultures that were ethnocentric and intolerant. Both recognized the validity and desirability of the conquest of enemies and their lands. The worldviews of both rejected racial equality. Both would have preferred the total elimination of the other from the Great Plains. To that end, both challenged the other's presence on the Great Plains through warfare, and occasionally, persons from both men's societies advocated and practiced ethnic extermination.[35]

There were also men of both cultures—peace chiefs, soldiers, and Indian agency personnel—who worked for peace, although U.S. policy by the late nineteenth century prescribed only Indian assimilation, not peaceful coexistence based on Indian independence. But on balance, the cultural gulf between Indian and non-Indian people was insurmountable. Overall the wars between Southern Cheyennes and non-Indian people in the 1860s and 1870s demonstrate a lack of willingness of many, and perhaps most, people on both sides to compromise and coexist in separate but equal worlds. The cultural dichotomy between capitalism and migratory hunting is not easily resolved when two cultures require opposing environmental conditions in order to function. Environmental definitions are viewed as natural and good by the culture whose view determines the future of the land, and with contempt by opposing cultures. Within a winner-take-all worldview, brutal acts of violence committed by opposing sides are bound to occur.

From the realist perspective, there is little in the written record of original sources, either white or Cheyenne, save Platten's account, to indicate that the Sappa Creek fight was an indiscriminate massacre of defenseless people who did not have a chance to surrender. There is only one white source—Platten—to support the notion that Sappa Creek was a genocidal event where atrocities were committed after the fighting ceased, or that Henely or any of his men displayed any unacceptable military conduct. The realist is not likely to recognize ambiguous Cheyenne oral history that has been passed down over many generations, ostensibly arguing that material may have been reshaped with changing political and social climates of successive generations. But in the analysis of the few available, heavily one-sided, and thus not strictly conclusive testimonies of those who were at Sappa Creek on that fateful April day in 1875, historians of the secondary sources, such as G. Derek West, have largely missed the symbolic power and significance of an event like the Sappa Creek episode.

Perhaps for the relativist, and more certainly for the Southern Cheyennes, the specific documented circumstances of the deaths of Little Bull's people are not significant beyond trying to convince non-Indians of the U.S. military's brutality toward Indians in the nineteenth century. From the Cheyenne perspective, among those people in Little Bull's camp who did not escape during the fighting but rather stood and fought to the death, the fact remains that women and children *were* killed, and perhaps even more women and children were killed than adult males. Lieutenant Henely himself attested in his official report to women and children being killed. It matters little at what specific time they died, for Henely took no prisoners. For the Cheyennes, the Sappa Creek fight was a massacre of far-reaching cultural significance. As with Wounded Knee on the northern plains, the Sappa Creek Massacre gives similar and symbolic closure to that part of Southern Cheyenne history dealing with the wars with the whites, a contest the Cheyennes could not win against the much larger population and enormous resources of the expansionist United States.

The annihilation of Little Bull's village at Sappa Creek is, like Wounded Knee, representative in its finality of the tragic experience the Southern Cheyenne people suffered at the end of their independent life on the plains. At both Sappa Creek and Wounded Knee there may have been a chance for peaceful resolution. Both the Cheyennes in 1875 and the Lakotas in 1890 were seeking refuge from what they feared would be punishment for what whites considered unacceptable transgressions. Arguments may be advanced in both cases that the killing of Indian people was both unjustifiably excessive and indiscriminate, regardless of the events that led to the initial shooting. In many ways Sappa Creek is the final fulfillment of Sweet Medicine's prophecy and *Esevone*'s desecration. It symbolizes the ultimate total conquest and dominion by a technological society with unlimited resources of a hunter-gatherer culture whose resources and life-sustaining natural environment have been taken to the brink of destruction. But the Sappa Creek story also symbolizes the survival of a proud people who today remember their history perhaps more than during any other time in recent decades.

The Sappa Creek Massacre is but one tragic example of how race dominated historical events on the central southern Great Plains to 1875. Race and racism cannot be separated from the theme of conquest. Conquest of the American West meant environmental control and defining the nature of the environment according to economic need. For Indian peoples, environmental control was driven in part by the need to possess natural resources like the buffalo, which sustained individual life and tribal tradition. For white culture, conquest of land and resources was not only driven by the forces of public policy but also, at the lowest level of implementation, by the personal ambitions of young military officers like Austin Henely, for whom promotion and financial gain was measured by experience in combat with Indians. That battles were fought that perhaps never should have been fought was the inevitable result of such a competitive climate.

Viewing the goals of both Indians and non-Indians from a presentist perspective in a continuous, often divisive, search for good and evil, or trying to illustrate the contributions of both groups in order to paint an oversimplified picture of western diversity can be misleading. Domination of the land by one race to the exclusion of the other race was the goal during the 1860s and 1870s. In an often-frustrating search for historical trends and models that define the American West as unique, one cannot escape the themes of race and conquest in shaping western history. The reality, of course, is that race and conquest make the West anything but unique. Rather, the West is part of the global trend throughout much of the nineteenth century that worked for the subordination of more technologically primitive, usually nonwhite societies, by first world imperialistic societies seeking to control world industrial resources and labor. For one of these conquered peoples, the Southern Cheyennes of the central southern plains of the United States, such is the tragic legacy of the Sappa Creek Massacre.

Notes

1. Henely's Report, 91.

2. Ibid. Interpreting Cheyenne art is a skill requiring the interpreter to have much knowledge of Cheyenne culture and how it is depicted in Cheyenne art, especially the knowledge of personal name glyphs usually connected by a dotted line to a warrior in the central focus of a drawing. Analyzing ledger drawings by identifying the enemy whites represented is even more difficult. Henely probably possessed no such knowledge. His interpretations are thus faulty. For example, the destruction of Major Lyman's wagons is usually credited to Comanches, not Cheyennes. Often ledger art is the only truly original archival documentation we have for certain events in Cheyenne history from the warriors' personal viewpoints. For detailed analyses of Cheyenne ledger art, see Joyce M. Szabo, *Howling Wolf and the History of Ledger Art* (Albuquerque: University of New Mexico Press, 1994) and Jean Afton, David Fridtjof Halaas, and Andrew E. Masich, with Richard N. Ellis, *Cheyenne Dog Soldiers: A Ledgerbook History of Coups and Combat* (Niwot: University Press of Colorado, 1997), which depicts the exploits of the Dog Soldier military society. The Dog Soldier ledger book was taken from the Summit Springs battlefield in 1869. Only recently have the events depicted been correlated with the year 1865—thus the difficulty in interpreting such ledger books.

3. Wheeler, *Buffalo Days*, 107.

4. Henely's Report, 90–91.

5. Platten's Account, 12.

6. Robbins's Account, 199.

7. George Bent in Hyde, *Life of George Bent*, 369.

8. Henely's Report, 91.

9. Wheeler, *Buffalo Days*, 107.

10. Platten's Account, 12.

11. Wheeler, *Buffalo Days*, 108.

12. Platten's Account, 12.

13. Robbins's Account, 199.

14. Ibid.

15. Wilson is quoted in Street, "Cheyenne Indian Massacre," 371.

16. George Bent to George Hyde, New Haven, Connecticut, September 5, 1914, May 11, 1915, and May 11, 1917, William Robertson Coe Collection, Beinecke Rare Book and Manuscript Library, Yale University, New Haven Connecticut. Powell, Sweet Medicine, 2:866–867.

17. Powell, People of the Sacred Mountain, 2:1357–1358 n. 11.

18. Sandoz, Cheyenne Autumn, 90–91, 93.

19. Historians Richard Slotkin and Richard White have made much about how the yellow journalists of this era used the theme of Indian "savagery" as a parallel to labor radicalism, and thus played on Gilded Age society's desire to suppress both. Slotkin and White draw heavily on the Custer myth. For a concise overview, see Richard White, It's Your Misfortune and None of My Own: A New History of the American West (Norman: University of Oklahoma Press, 1991), 622.

20. For an examination of settlers' perceptions of Indians in western Kansas during the 1860s and 1870s, see Miner, West of Wichita, 14–25, 109–118. A frequent concern of settlers during these years was an insufficient U.S. military presence.

21. The historian who has made the most of the theme of the frontier nostalgia that gripped many Americans during the early 1900s is Robert G. Athern. See his The Mythic West in the Twentieth Century (Lawrence: University Press of Kansas, 1986), 1–42.

22. An interesting example of this changing Progressive era journalism may be found in the same volume as contains Street's article on the Sappa Creek Massacre. Immediately following Street's account in this collection is an ethnological study of the Kaw Indians. See Joab Spencer, "The Kaw or Kansas Indians: Their Customs, Manners, and Folk-Lore," Transactions of the Kansas Historical Society 10 (1907–1908): 373–380. Street's and Spencer's articles were grouped under a heading on the volume title page nostalgically titled "The Disappearing Indians." Ironically, the category was listed next to one titled "The Soldiers of Kansas."

23. Lockard, "The Battle of Achilles," 30.

24. Sandoz's depiction of the Sappa Creek Massacre in Cheyenne Autumn is one example of interpreting causality for the Dull Knife raids. For a different viewpoint see Ramon Powers, "The Northern Cheyenne Trek Through Western Kansas in 1878: Frontiersmen, Indians, and Cultural Conflict," The Trail Guide 17, nos. 3–4 (September 1972).

25. Street, "Cheyenne Indian Massacre," 372–373.

26. Kansas State Historical Society, "The Last of the Rank and File," xviii.

27. William D. Street, "Incidents of the Dull Knife Raid," Notes of William D. Street, Kansas State Historical Society, Topeka, Kansas, 2.

28. F. M. Lockard, The History of the Early Settlement of Norton County, Kansas (Norton, Kans.: Champion Press, 1894), 205.

29. Lockard, The Battle of Achilles, 29.

30. Will Kenyon, "The Last Raid of Spotted Horse."

31. Wheeler, *Buffalo Days*, 108–110.

32. Research files, part 2, pp. 14–18, Mari Sandoz Papers, Special Collections and Manuscripts Division, University of Nebraska Library, Lincoln, Nebraska.

33. Hyde, *Life of George Bent*, v. A precious few words from Bent to Hyde regarding peripheral events at this time were included in letters on file in Yale's Coe collection.

34. Jones, "Curse of Ta-Kanah," 49–50.

35. Bent in particular speaks of the Cheyenne annihilating a war party of Pawnees between the forks of the Platte in about 1833, as well as several other instances where the plains tribes exterminated their enemies in battle. See Hyde, *Life of George Bent*, 48–49.

ChapterVII

Epilogue

Amache Prower's prediction of Lieutenant Austin Henely's untimely death came to pass, although the event took closer to three years, rather than one. While campaigning against Apaches near Fort Bowie, Arizona Territory, in 1878, Henely met his end. During the summer of that year elements of the 6th Cavalry built a supply camp in the juniper hills of the lower Chiricahua Mountains near the Mexican border. Camp Supply was to serve as a temporary base to be used to aid the army in intercepting small bands of Chiricahua Apaches returning to the United States from Sonora and Chihuahua. Because of diplomatic considerations, U.S. troops always had trouble crossing the international border in pursuit of warring Apaches.

On July 11, 1878, the usually benign mountain stream running near the supply camp flooded, as often happens in the southern Arizona mountains during the summer storm season. Soon a raging flood swept through the camp, where men from several companies of the 6th Cavalry were bivouacked. One of their officers was First Lieutenant Austin Henely (he had been promoted November 15, 1876), commander of D Company. The other officer at the camp was Second Lieutenant John A. Rucker. While in Arizona Henely was reunited with Rucker, one of his West Point classmates and friends, an influential friend indeed, for Rucker's sister, Irene, was married to the commander of the Division of the Missouri, General Philip Sheridan.[1] Henely mounted his horse and naively plunged into the torrent to assist other men in rescuing ration packages that were quickly being submerged by the flood.[2]

About 7:00 P.M. Henely's horse stumbled in the stream, throwing Henely into the rapids; his head struck a tree, rendering him unconscious. Rucker plunged into the torrent in an attempt to save the unconscious Henely. When some of the troopers saw Rucker's horse reach shore a few minutes later without its rider, they knew both men had likely drowned.[3] That night Rucker's body was discovered downstream about a mile from the camp. The next morning a search party found Henely's body sixty yards from where Rucker's had washed ashore.[*][4]

Upon hearing of her son's death, Henely's mother, Mrs. Delia Callihan, wrote to the adjutant general from her home in Chicago. After her second husband's death she had become almost financially destitute. "When my husband died," she wrote, "I had to fall back on part of poor Austin's salary that he cheerfully gave. But it caused me many a pang to take it as I knew he needed it himself & now I think you can see into my situation. I hope you will forward to me anything that was coming to him, and also his effects."[5] Four months later Mrs. Callihan still had not received her son's property. Some of Henely's effects reached the War Department in Washington, D.C., nearly a year after his death.[6] Both Henely and Rucker were buried in the post cemetery at Fort Bowie, Arizona Territory.[7]

The United States, upon Henely's recommendation prior to his death, awarded eight Medals of Honor to men of H Company, 6th Cavalry for action at Sappa Creek on April 23, 1875. Decorations were awarded to Sergeants Frederick Platten and Richard L. Tea; Trumpeter Michael Dawson; and Privates James F. Ayres, Peter W. Gardner, Simpson Hornaday, James Louthers, and Marcus M. Robbins. Originally Henely had recommended decorations for Chaplain William W. Morris, Private Patrick J. Coyle, and Homer Wheeler,

---

[*] Today the small stream in the Chiricahua Mountains where Henely and Rucker drowned is named Rucker Creek. The author can attest to the stream's ferocity during periods of flash floods, for he had a narrow escape during one in the 1970s while exploring in Rucker Canyon near his home. W. H. Carter discusses the flood potential of innocent-looking western streams. He claims that during the 1870s more Army officers died from drowning than did Navy officers during the same period. See Carter, *From Yorktown to Santiago with the Sixth Cavalry,* 199.

the Fort Wallace post trader. But after Henely made more formal recommendations in 1876, Coyle was eliminated because he had deserted a month after the Sappa Creek fight. Morris was denied because he had already won a Medal of Honor in the Red River War. Wheeler was also denied because at the time of the Sappa Creek fight he was a civilian and therefore not eligible for a Medal of Honor.[8] In giving his final endorsement, General Pope replied by writing: "The officer (Henely) who makes this recommendation is himself entitled to the highest consideration for his conduct in this affair in which he was in command."[9]

During the 1870s the Medal of Honor was the only decoration the United States awarded for valor. Accordingly, the medal was handed out more liberally than it is today. Nevertheless, even by the standards of the nineteenth century, the reasons given for some of the recommendations are questionable. In other cases no reasons were given. Henely, for example, only listed the names of those recommended accompanied by a short citation to the adjutant general:

Sir:

I have the honor to recommend that for Conspicuous Courage, unusual activity, and for service rendered beyond the ordinary duty of a soldier, in an engagement with hostile Indians April 23rd, 1875, in Northern Kansas, Medals of honor be awarded to the following officers* and men.[10]

Henely listed no details pertaining to the individual acts of valor.

Considering the circumstances and allegations of massacre at both Wounded Knee and Sappa Creek, the proportionate number of awards for valor for both events seems excessive and unwarranted by today's standards. Eight Medals of Honor were awarded for Sappa Creek. Twenty Medals of Honor were awarded for Wounded Knee, a much larger action. At Wounded

---

* The "officers" Henely refers to is Homer Wheeler, who was commissioned a second lieutenant in the 5th Cavalry in October 1876, at the time of the recommendation. He was a civilian, however, at the time of the Sappa Creek engagement.

Knee some of the individual acts of valor cited by recommending officers included such dubious things as "conspicuous bravery for bringing to the skirmish line a stampeded pack mule," and "bravery displayed while shooting hostile Indians." Several awards were granted for "exposing himself to the enemy."[11]

In 1916 the U.S. Congress required the War Department to review the 2,625 Medals of Honor awarded to that date. A few were rescinded because they had gone to civilians. In another case 864 medals were rescinded from men of the 27th Maine Volunteer Infantry who served during the Civil War because the medals had been awarded as an inducement to reenlist. In 1917 standards were tightened requiring "conspicuous gallantry or intrepidity at the risk of life above and beyond the call of duty."[12] The review board rescinded none of the Wounded Knee or Sappa Creek medals in 1916. Over the years the question of rescinding the Wounded Knee medals surfaces periodically. To date no one has made a meaningful effort to rescind medals awarded for Sappa Creek.[13]

The lives of other major players in the Sappa Creek story can be traced past 1875. Homer Wheeler, upon the recommendation of General Pope, received a commission in the 5th Cavalry as a second lieutenant for his services at Sappa Creek. He entered the army in October 1875 and served in the Great Sioux War the next year. He participated in the destruction of Dull Knife's Northern Cheyenne winter camp on November 25, 1876.[14] Sergeant Frederick Platten, for all his later animosity toward Henely, served two enlistments in H Company, 6th Cavalry. Later he served as an army packer. He remained in Arizona, where he passed away at the age of eighty-four on March 2, 1939. His reminiscences and accusations against Henely were published twenty years later, in 1959, albeit through the editing of his largely oral testimony by Thomas E. Way.[15] Private Marcus M. Robbins likewise would remain in the 6th Cavalry, and he was promoted to sergeant. We will probably never know when George Bent's informant, Blind Bull, related his account of the Sappa Creek tragedy to Bent, but it had to be prior to Bent's death in 1918. Bent's letters to George Hyde pertaining to peripheral information about Sappa Creek, however, are dated between 1914 and 1917.

The cause célèbre for troops in the Red River War, and undoubtedly for the soldiers at Sappa Creek, was the killing by Medicine Water's war party in 1874 of the John German family. Second Lieutenant C. C. Hewitt fought at Sappa Creek a year after recovering the bodies of the German family. Medicine Water, Chief of the Bowstring Society, was incarcerated as a prisoner of war in the federal penitentiary at Fort Marion, Florida, in 1875. He returned to Clinton, Oklahoma, with the other Cheyenne prisoners at Fort Marion in 1878. He died in Oklahoma in 1926. Others were not so lucky. Grey Beard, who saw to the safety of the German sisters, was killed by a guard in Mississippi while on his way to Fort Marion. Medicine Water's wife, Buffalo Calf Woman, who split John German's head with an ax, was also incarcerated at Fort Marion. While she was there, one of the guards described her as "a fine looking Indian woman but was as mean as they come."[16] She died in Oklahoma in 1881 at the age of forty-one. She and her husband are buried side by side in an unmarked grave in Oklahoma. At the time of their incarceration their children were left at Darlington Agency to be schooled in the ways of the whites.[17]

The surviving German sisters lived long lives. Catherine went to California after she married Amos Swerdfeger and died there in 1932. Julia and Addie graduated from Sabetha (Kansas) High School. Addie attended the University of Kansas and later married Frank Andrews, a farmer from Bern, Kansas. She bore him eleven children. Julia married Howard Reese, and then Albert Brooks. She moved to California, where she died in 1959, the last surviving German sister. Sophia married Albert Feldmann, a farmer. They spent most of their lives on a farm near Humboldt, Nebraska. Sophia died in 1947.[18]

In July 1989, one of Sophia German Feldmann's descendants, a great-great granddaughter named Arlene Jauken, contacted the Oklahoma Historical Society seeking information about the German Massacre. Her letter was forwarded to a historical researcher named John L. Sipes. What resulted was a fantastic bit of historical irony coming full circle after more than a century. John Sipes was the great-great grandson of Medicine Water and Buffalo Calf Woman. Sipes telephoned Jauken on August 1, 1989, to inform her of who he was and that he had been assigned to respond to her letter. "I was so shocked," Jauken said. "He called me early in the morning and said, 'I'm the descendant of Medicine Water and Buffalo Calf Woman who killed your great-great grandparents.' "[19]

The next year, on September 9, 1990, John L. Sipes of Norman, Oklahoma, and Arlene Feldmann Jauken of Troutdale, Oregon, shared the speaker's podium for a German Family–Cheyenne peace ceremony on the site of the German Massacre, six miles northwest of Russell Springs, Kansas. The ceremony was organized by Sipes, Jauken, and Leslie Linville, a local historian long interested in the German Massacre. A closed Cheyenne ceremonial preceded the speeches. Before the ceremony, both Sipes and Jauken made statements to the press regarding the long-ago event that had so crystallized public opinion during the Red River War. "Kansas was the home of the Cheyennes," Sipes said. "That was their land. They fought the Pawnee, the Kaw, the Osage, anybody who crossed it." Medicine Water and Buffalo Calf Woman saw so much brutality, "they declared war and they went to war." Sipes related how both his great-great grandparents had been at Sand Creek and had lost members of both their families to Chivington's volunteers. The families of John German, Medicine Water, and Buffalo Calf Woman were victims of that war between whites and Cheyennes. So too were Little Bull's followers at Sappa Creek.[20]

Sipes and Jauken did not cast blame or look for easy explanations defined in terms of universal good versus evil. The Cheyennes blessed those participating in the peace ceremonial. Arlene Jauken wrote at the top of her program, "The German Girls would say, 'Forgiveness,' and 'Peace to all mankind.' "[21]

Notes

1. Henely's ACP File; Altshuler, *Cavalry Yellow and Infantry Blue*, 289.

2. W. H. Carter, *From Yorktown to Santiago with the Sixth U.S. Cavalry* (Austin, Tex.: State House Press, 1989), 198.

3. Carter, *From Yorktown to Santiago with the Sixth U.S. Cavalry*, 198.

4. Henely's ACP File.

5. Mrs. Delia Callihan to adjutant general's office, August 4, 1878, letter in Henely's ACP File; Johnson, "Austin Henely," 12.

6. Johnson, "Austin Henely," 12.

7. Carter, *From Yorktown to Santiago with the Sixth U.S. Cavalry,* 198–199.

8. Copies of original recommendations are in Henely's ACP File. For printed copies of the same documents see also AGO File 2815-1876 in Joe F. Taylor, "The Indian Campaign on the Staked Plains, 1874–1875," *Panhandle-Plains Historical Review* 35 (1962): 229–235.

9. Ibid.

10. Ibid.

11. For an evaluative discussion of these medals, see Jerry Green, "The Medals of Wounded Knee," *Nebraska History* 75, no. 2 (summer 1994): 200–208.

12. Ibid.

13. Ibid.

14. Wheeler, *Buffalo Days,* 111, 130–147.

15. Platten's Account, 2.

16. Sipes's List.

17. Although it is not a scholarly work, for an interesting synopsis of Medicine Water's and Buffalo Calf Woman's later lives taken from interviews with Oklahoma Cheyennes living today, see Patrick M. Mendoza, *Song of Sorrow: Massacre at Sand Creek* (Denver: Willow Wind Publishing Co., 1993), 164.

18. Miscellaneous German family papers. Copies on file in the Wray Museum, Wray, Colorado.

19. From the *Gazette Telegraph,* Colorado Springs, Colorado. Quoted in Mendoza, *Song of Sorrow,* 163.

20. *The Salina Journal,* August 6, 1990.

21. German Family–Cheyenne Peace Ceremonial program brochure. Copy on file in the Wray Museum, Wray, Colorado.

Henely's Official Report of the Battle of Sappa Creek

The Assistant Adjutant-General,
  Department of the Missouri, Fort Leavenworth, Kans.

Fort Wallace, Kans. April 26, 1875

Sir: I have the honor to submit the following report of operations performed in compliance with Special Orders No. 38, dated Headquarters Fort Wallace, Kans., April 18, 1875.

On the morning of the 19th of April, with forty men of H Company, Sixth Cavalry, Lieut. C.C. Hewitt, Nineteenth Infantry, engineer officer, Acting Assistant Surgeon F. H. Atkins, and Mr. Homer Wheeler, post-trader of Fort Wallace, as guide, fifteen days' rations, ten days' forage, and six-mule teams, I started for Punished Woman's Fork to strike the trail of a party of Indians reported there.

My transportation, all that was at Fort Wallace, was so inadequate that I made only thirteen miles that day. The next day I directed my wagons, with a suitable guard, under command of Sergeant Kitchen, to proceed directly to Hackberry Creek, while I scouted Twin Butte and hackberry to find a trail. Corporal Morris, commanding the advance, about noon discovered a trail of twelve lodges. I then hunted up my wagons, abandoned one wagon and

Source: *Report of the Secretary of War for the Year 1875*, 44th Cong., 1st sess., 1876, H. Doc. 1.

half my forage, rations and camp-equipage, notified the commanding officer at Fort Wallace of the fact, in order that they might be recovered, and
started on the trail, at the rate of nearly five miles an hour, reaching the
Smoky Hill River that night.

During the night it rained, and the trail was followed with difficulty the
next day to the Kansas Pacific Railroad, near Monument Station.

The Indians scattered after crossing the road, and a single trail was followed for several miles when it was lost entirely. I then struck directly for
the headwaters of the Solomon River, camped on it that night, and deliber-
ated with Lieutenant Hewitt, Dr. Atkins, and Mr. Wheeler as to the best course
to pursue. Three plans were proposed. One was to turn back and try and
strike some one of the other bands that we had reason to believe were crossing north. Another to strike Sappa Creek, follow it for a day or two, and then
march south to Grinnel Station, and if we failed to find a trail on Sappa, we
still had a chance to strike one of the other bands, which might strike the
Kansas Pacific near Grinnel. The last plan, and the one that was finally adopted,
was to march in a northeast course to the North Beaver and follow it to its
head, as it was believed the Indians would collect there, and follow it down
for the purpose of hunting.

Shortly after daylight a hunters' trail was discovered, which was followed until we met a party of hunters, who informed me that the Indians I
was after were on the North Fork of Sappa Creek, and had robbed their
camp the day before while they were absent, and that they were going into
Wallace, as they had reason to believe the Indians would attack them. Three
of the hunters, Henry Campbell, Charles Schroeder, and Samuel B. Srach,
volunteered to conduct me to the vicinity of the Indian camp, which they
thought was about seventeen miles from where I met them. We marched
about six miles and camped in a ravine until sundown, then the march was
continued to within about five miles of Sappa Creek.

I then halted and went into camp on the prairie, and the three hunters,
accompanied by Mr. Wheeler, started to find the camp. Their efforts were
successful, and we arrived at the North Fork of Sappa Creek in the gray
dawn of the morning, about three-quarters of a mile above the camp, guided
by the sight of a number of ponies grazing. I could not immediately dis-

cover the camp, as I could not tell whether it was above or below the herd. Mr. Wheeler, who had ridden off some distance to the right, galloped furiously back swinging his hat and shouting at the top of his voice. I immediately galloped toward him with my command, and the camp was displayed to view.

My plan for the attack had been arranged as follows: Sergeant Kitchen was detailed with ten men to surround the herd, kill the herders, round it up as near to the main command as possible, stay in charge of it with half his men, and send the rest to join me. Corporal Sharples, with five men, was left with the wagon, with instructions to keep as near me as the very rugged and broken nature of the country would permit, always occupying high ground. With the rest of my command I intended to intrude myself between the Indians and their herd and attack them if they did not surrender.

I will state here that the North Fork of the Sappa at this point is exceedingly crooked, is bordered by high and precipitous bluffs, and flows sluggishly through a marshy bottom, making it difficult to reach, and almost impossible to cross. As we charged down the side of the bluff I could see about ten or twelve indians running rapidly up the bluff to a small herd of ponies—others escaped down the creek to another herd, while the remainder, the last to be awakened probably, seeing that they could not escape, prepared for a desperate defense. By this time I had reached the creek, which looked alarmingly deep and marshy. Knowing that no time was to be lost in hunting a crossing, I plunged in with my horse, Mr. Wheeler with me. By extraordinary efforts our horses floundered through. A corporal, who followed, became mired, but by desperate efforts all managed to cross, just as a number of dusky figures with long rifles confronted us, their heads appearing over a peculiarly-shaped bank, made so by the creek in high water. This bank, with the portion of the creek and bluffs in the immediate vicinity, possess remarkable topographical features, and I will endeavor to describe them. As we approach the creek from the south it is observed that it makes a sharp bend to the northeast, and then turns south for a short distance. The ground slopes from the top of the ridge to near the creek, where it terminates abruptly in a semicircular crest concave toward it, and about five feet above another small slope which terminates at the creek. We crossed the creek at the termination of the southern arc; the Indian camp was at its northern termination. A number of holes dug in the ground were on the chord of the arc. Some of the indians took refuge in these holes—others lined the banks with their rifles resting on the crest. I formed my men rapidly into line and motioned the Indians to come in, as did Mr. Wheeler, who was on my left and a few feet in advance. One Indian, who appeared to be a chief, made some rapid gesticulations, which I at first thought was for a parley, but soon discovered it was directed to those in the rear. I gave the command to fight on foot, which was obeyed with extraordinary prompt- ness. As the men dismounted the Indians fired, but excitedly. Fortunately no one was hit. I then ordered my men to fire and posted them around the crest in skirmish-line. If we imagine a dress-circle of a theater to be lowered to within about five feet of the pit, the men to be deployed about the edge and the Indians down among the orchestra chairs, it will give some idea of our relative positions. The most exposed part was near the center of the arc, corresponding to that part of the dress-circle opposite the entrance. Here Sergeant Theodore Papier and Private Robert Theims, Company H, Sixth Cavalry, were instantly killed while fighting with extraordinary courage. They did not appear to be more than 15 or 20 feet from the Indians when they fell. After firing for about twenty minutes, and the Indians having ceased firing, I withdrew my men and their horses for the purpose of pursuing the Indians who had escaped. Hardly had we mounted when two Indians ran up to the two bodies, which had been carried some distance up the ridge. I immediately detached three or four men at a gallop to charge them, and the Indians retreated, accomplishing nothing. Just then an Indian, gaudily decked, jumped from a hole, and with peculiar side-long leaps attempted to escape, which he did not. I then posted my men at the two ends of the crest, avoid- ing the center, and began again, the Indians returning the fire from their holes without any damage for some time when the firing again ceased and I concluded all were dead.

Seeing a herd of ponies on the hill behind me, I sent two men to bring them in. A number of Indians tried to cut them off. I mounted and went to their assistance, driving the Indians off and bringing in the herd. Coming back to burn the camp, a solitary shot was fired from the holes, striking the horse of Trumpeter Dawson through the body. I then concluded to make a

sure finish, ordering Corporal Morris with a detachment to advance to the edge of the crest, keeping up a continual fire, so that the Indians would not dare to show themselves above the crest; another detachment went to the left and rear, and all advanced together; some few shots were fired from the holes without any damage. Nearly all the Indians by this time were dead; occasionally a wounded Indian would thrust the barrel of a rifle from one of the holes and fire, discovering himself to be dispatched.

I have not been able to determine the original object of these holes or pits, but judge they were originally made for the shelter of those Indians who had no lodges, and were deepened and enlarged during the fight.

Nineteen dead warriors were counted; eight squaws and children were unavoidably killed by shots intended for the warriors. From the war-bonnets and rich ornaments, I judged two were chiefs, and one whose bonnet was surmounted by two horns, to be a medicine-man. The Indians were nearly all armed with rifles and carbines, the Spencer carbine predominating. A number of muzzle-loading rifles, and one Springfield breech-loading rifle, musket caliber .50, were found.

I then burned all their lodges and effects and threw some of the arms into the fire, destroying also a quantity of ammunition. There were twelve lodges, five or six covered with skins, and the other were frames, composed of new hackberry poles. Eight rifles and carbines were brought to the post of Fort Wallace and have been turned in.

I then withdrew with the captured stock, numbering 134 animals, to my wagon, which I could discern during the whole fight on a high bluff about a mile distant. I judge the fight lasted about three hours. Feeling certain that other bands were in the vicinity who would soon concentrate and attack me, and at least recapture the stock, I marched to Monument Station, thirty-eight miles distant, reaching it about 8 o'clock next morning. The march was continued to Sheridan Station that day, where we were overtaken by a terrible norther, and I was forced to camp under a bank. The storm was so severe that it was impossible to herd the captured stock, our whole attention being directed to save ourselves and horses from freezing to death. After a night of intense suffering among horses and men, the men having but one blanket each, and no tents—some of the men being frozen, and the

others who had dug holes in the bank for shelter, requiring to be dug out of the snow by their comrades—the storm abated and we split up in small squads to search for the captured stock. After a wearisome ride, occupying nearly all day, in which the faces and eyes of the men were injured by the reflection of the sun from the snow to such an extent as to necessitate medical treatment, eighty-nine ponies, one horse (branded M, and recognized by some of the men as having been ridden by Private Pettyjohn, Company M, Sixth Cavalry, who was killed on McClellan Creek, Texas), seven mules, and one Spanish burro were recovered. Some of the rest may have perished by the storm, and some I believe will be picked up by citizens who have started, I understand, in search of them. One thing is certain, they will never be of service to the Indians.

I cannot find words to express the courage, patience, endurance, and intelligence exhibited by all under my command. Lieut. C. C. Hewitt, Nineteenth Infantry, although by his duties not required to be at the front, was under fire continually, exhibited great courage, and performed important service. Dr. F. H. Atkins gave proof of the greatest courage and fortitude, going up on the bodies of Sergeant Papier and Private Theims to examine them, when such action appeared to be almost certain death; and again during the terrible suffering amidst the storm of the 25th, he was cheerful and full of words of encouragement to us all, exhibiting the greatest nerve when the stoutest heart despaired.

I respectfully recommend that Doctor Atkins's important services receive the consideration to which they are entitled. All of the men behaved with great gallantly [sic]. The following deserve special mention: Sergeant Richard L. Tea, Sergeant Frederick Platten, Corporal William M. Morris, Trumpeter Michael Dawson, Privates James F. Ayres, Patrick J. Coyle, James Lowthers, Markus [sic] M. Robbins, Simpson Hornady, and Peter W. Gardner, all of Company H, Sixth Cavalry.

Mr. Homer W. Wheeler, post trader of Fort Wallace, left his business and volunteered to accompany the detachment as a guide. His knowledge of the country and of Indian habits was of the utmost service. He risked his life to find the Indian camp; was the first to discover it in the morning, and although not expected to take part in the fight, was always on the skirmish-

line, and showed the greatest courage and activity. The three hunters, Henry Campbell, Charles Schroeder, and Samuel B. Srack [sic], who, with Mr. Wheeler, found the camp, performed important services; they participated in a portion of the fight and drove in a herd of ponies, which otherwise would not have been captured. When these men turned back with me, I promised that they would be suitably rewarded if they found the camp. I respectfully request that their services, as well as those of Mr. Wheeler, be substantially acknowledged.

I brought to the post, for interment with the honors of war, the bodies of Sergeant Papier and Private Theims.

Although none were wounded, a number of the men had balls pass through their clothing, and one ball passed through the cartridge-box (which had been moved to the front) of Private Patrick Coyle.

One horse was abandoned, having been lamed; another was shot in the engagement, and fifteen are now temporarily unserviceable, rendered so by the storm; nearly all of the men require medical treatment for the same reason.

There was found in the camp of the Indians a memorandum-book containing rude though expressive sketches, made by themselves, of their exploits. Among a great number were the following, as I interpret them: The charge on the scouts at the battle of Red River; the attack on Adobe Walls and on Major Lyman's train; the killing of Private Pettyjohn, and another (of which I am not certain) representing the murder of the Germain [sic] family.

The following has been demonstrated to my entire satisfaction on this trip:

1st. The security of horses tied to the picket-line by one of the fore feet. For the first night my horses (nearly all new ones) became frightened and made a desperate effort to stampede, which I believe would have been successful had they been tied by the halter-shank.

2nd. That a short stout strap attached to the halter and terminated by a strap is better to link horses than tying them with the reins while fighting on foot.

Very respectfully,
AUSTIN HENELY,
Second Lieut. Sixth Cavalry.

Bibliography

The primary sources for the Sappa Creek Massacre begin with Henely's account found in the *Report of the Secretary of War for the Year 1875*, and reproduced in the appendix of this book. Hencly's Appointment, Commission and Personal file is located among the military records of the National Archives in Washington, D.C., and the file is now on microfiche. The file contains correspondence concerning Henely's promotions, assignments, and his sick call reports while a cadet at West Point. It also contains correspondence concerning the circumstances of his death, as well as correspondence from his mother to the adjutant general. A perusal of RG 393 in the Records of U.S. Army Continental Commands yielded no additional insight into the Sappa Creek fight save Lieutenant C. C. Hewitt's logistical estimates.

Robbins's account is found in Beyer and Keydel's *Deeds of Valor*. Although it was recorded after Platten's death by Thomas E. Way and is suggestive of embellishment, Platten's account is found in Way's *Sgt. Fred Platten's Ten Years on the Trail of the Redskins*.

The main Cheyenne source for the Sappa Creek fight is found in the final chapter of George E. Hyde's *Life of George Bent Written from His Letters*. Some of Bent's letters between 1914 and 1917 to George Hyde detailing peripheral events are located in the Coe Collection of the Yale University Library. Although Bent's account is filtered through the eyes of George Hyde, Bent, a mixed-blood Cheyenne formally schooled in Westport,

Missouri, was fluent in English and Cheyenne. Hyde always regarded Bent as a reliable informant. Bent's letters demonstrate his ability to transfer Cheyenne oral tradition from the Cheyenne language into English without losing meaning. Hyde's book is not as agenda-driven as some oral translations recorded by white ethnologists. In addition, Bent knew enough English to keep Hyde on the narrow track. Whether he actually proofread Hyde's original manuscript, however, is not known.

Perusals of traditional manuscript collections such as the Eli S. Ricker Papers in the Nebraska State Historical Society, the Walter M. Camp Papers at Brigham Young University, the Joseph G. Masters Collection in the Kansas State Historical Society, and the George B. Grinnell Papers in the Southwest Museum yielded no additional original material from the sources cited herein.

Margot Liberty details how Indian historical accounts almost always are concerned with individual exploits rather than with the big picture of overall events. See Margot Liberty, "Oral and Written Perspectives on the Indian Wars," in Charles E. Rankin, ed., *Legacy: New Perspectives on the Battle of the Little Bighorn*, (Helena: Montana Historical Society Press, 1996). Such is the case with Bent's account of the Sappa Creek Massacre, which was related to him by Blind Bull. Some of the events Bent recounted, particularly the killing of White Bear, fill gaps in the military records in a logical and probable manner.

Although oral history passed down over many generations is subject to altered meaning through the years, the best secondary Cheyenne source based on Bent, Street, Lockard, Sandoz, and long-standing Cheyenne oral testimony related in the 1850s is Peter John Powell, *People of the Sacred Mountain: A History of the Northern Cheyenne Chiefs and Warrior Societies, 1830–1879 with an Epilogue, 1969–1974*.

A one-stop source for the records of the German family, who may have been major players in the later stages of the Red River War and the "stampede" north of several Cheyenne groups, one of which was Little Bull's ill-fated band, is the German family papers, copies of which are consolidated in the Wray Museum in Wray, Colorado.

GOVERNMENT DOCUMENTS

Adjutant General's Office. *Chronological List of Actions, &c.,With Indians from January 15, 1837 to January, 1891*. Washington D.C.: Government Printing Office, 1891.

National Archives. "Letters Received." RG 94. File 349-1874.

———. "Letters Received by Appointment, Commission, and Personal Branch," Adjutant General's Office, 1871–1894. RG 94. Microfiche publication M1395. Fiche ACP 000253.

———. "Letters Received, 1874–1882," U.S. Army Continental Commands. Box 9. RG 393.

———. Records of the Adjutant General's Office. RG 94. File 3490-1877.

U.S. House. *Annual Report of the Commissioner of Indian Affairs for the Year 1874*. 43rd Cong., 2nd sess., H. Doc. 1, pt. 5, vol. 6. Serial 1639.

———. *Annual Report of the Commissioner of Indian Affairs for the Year 1875*. 44th Cong., 1st sess., H. Doc. 1, pt. 5, vol. 4. Serial 1680.

———. *Annual Report of the Secretary of War for the Year 1875*. 44th Cong., 1st sess., H. Doc. 1, pt. 2, vol. 1. Serial 1674.

MANUSCRIPT COLLECTIONS

Baldwin, Frank. Diary of Lieutenant Frank Baldwin (photocopy). Wray Museum, Wray, Colorado.

Bent, George, and George E. Hyde. Correspondence. William Robertson Coe Collection. Beinecke Rare Book and Manuscript Library, Yale University, New Haven, Connecticut.

German, Adelaide. Correspondence. Kansas State Historical Society.

German Family. Papers. Wray Museum, Wray, Colorado.

German Family–Cheyenne Peace Ceremonial program brochure. Wray Museum, Wray, Colorado.

Sandoz, Mari. Papers. Research files, part 2. Special Collections and Manuscripts Division, University of Nebraska Library, Lincoln, Nebraska.

Sipes, John. List of Cheyenne participants in the German Massacre (photocopy). Wray Museum, Wray, Colorado.

Street, William D. Notes of William D. Street. Kansas State Historical Society.

Sutton, E. S. Unpublished manuscript. Rawlins County, Kansas Historical Society.

NEWSPAPERS

Colorado Springs Gazette Telegraph, Sep. 10, 1990.
Leavenworth (Kansas) Daily Times, Dec. 3, 1874.
Newton Kansan, Sep. 17, 1874.
Topeka Capitol, May 2, 1937.
Wichita Eagle, Aug. 13, 1874.
Salina (Kansas) Journal, Aug. 6, 1990.

PERIODICAL ARTICLES AND PUBLICATIONS OF LEARNED SOCIETIES

Green, Jerry. "The Medals of Wounded Knee." *Nebraska History* 75, no. 2 (summer 1994).

Hutton, Paul A. "Phil Sheridan's Frontier." *Montana:The Magazine of Western History* 38, no. 1 (winter 1988).

Johnson, Barry C. "Austin Henely: Center of the Sappa Creek Controversy." *English Westerners' Brand Book* 7, no. 3 (April 1965).

Jones, Gene. "Curse of Ta-Kanah." *Real West* 6, no. 29 (May 1963).

Kansas State Historical Society. "The Last of the Rank and File Whose Blood Drenched Kansas Soil." *Collections of the Kansas State Historical Society* 12 (1911–1912): addenda.

Kenyon, Will. "The Last Raid of Spotted Horse." *Sunday Magazine* (August 12, 1906). (Copy in "Indian Depredations and Battles, Clippings," vol. 1, Center for Historical Research, Kansas State Historical Society.)

Lockard, F. M. "The Battle of Achilles." *Kansas Magazine* 2, no. 1 (July 1909).

Montgomery, Mrs. F. C. "Fort Wallace and Its Relation to the Frontier." *Kansas Historical Collections* 17 (1926–1928).

———. "United States Surveyors Massacred by Indians." *Kansas Historical Quarterly*, no. 1 (1931).

Powers, Ramon. "The Northern Cheyenne Trek Through Western Kansas in 1878: Frontiersmen, Indians, and Cultural Conflict." *The Trail Guide* 17, nos. 3–4 (September 1972).

Smits, David D. "The Frontier Army and the Destruction of the Buffalo, 1865–1883." *Western Historical Quarterly* 25, no. 3 (autumn 1994).

Spencer, Joab. "The Kaw or Kansas Indians: Their Customs, Manners, and Folk-Lore." *Transactions of the Kansas Historical Society* 10 (1907–1908).

Street, William D. "Cheyenne Indian Massacre on the Middle Fork of the Sappa." *Transactions of the Kansas State Historical Society* 10, no. 4 (1907–1908).

Taylor, Joe F. "The Indian Campaign on the Staked Plains, 1874–1875." *Panhandle-Plains Historical Review* 35 (1962).

Thrapp, Dan. "Attack on Sappa Creek." *Frontier Times* 37, no. 1 (December-January 1963).

Webb, Bernice Larson. "First Homesteader and the Battle of Sappa Creek." *Kansas Quarterly* 10, no. 3 (summer 1978).

West, G. Derek. "The Battle of Sappa Creek, 1875." *Kansas Historical Quarterly* 34, no. 2 (summer 1968).

White, Lonnie J. "White Women Captives of the Southern Plains Indians, 1866–1875." *Journal of the West* 8, no. 3 (July 1969).

BOOKS

Afton, Jean, David Fridtjof Halaas, and Andrew E. Masich, with Richard N. Ellis. *Cheyenne Dog Soldiers: A Ledgerbook History of Coups and Combat*. Niwot: University Press of Colorado, 1997.

Altshuler, Constance Wynn, ed. *Cavalry Yellow and Infantry Blue: Army Officers in Arizona Between 1851 and 1886*. Tucson: Arizona Historical Society, 1991.

Athern, Robert. *The Mythic West in the Twentieth Century*. Lawrence: University Press of Kansas, 1986.

Berthrong, Donald J. *The Southern Cheyennes*. Norman: University of Oklahoma Press, 1963.

Beyer, W. F., and O. F. Keydel, eds. 2 vols. *Deeds of Valor*. Detroit: The Perrien Keydel Co., 1907.

Carter, R. G. *On the Border With Mackenzie or Winning West Texas from the Comanches*. New York: Antiquarian Press, Ltd., 1961.

Carter, W. H. *From Yorktown to Santiago with the Sixth U.S. Cavalry*. Austin, Tex.: State House Press, 1989.

Chalfant, William Y. *Cheyennes at Dark Water Creek: The Last Fight of the Red River War*. Norman: University of Oklahoma Press, 1997.

Cook, John R. *The Border and the Buffalo: The Untold Story of the Southwest Plains.* Topeka, Kans.: Crane and Co., 1907.

Dary, David A. *The Buffalo Book: The Saga of an American Symbol.* New York: Avon Books, 1974.

Dixon, Olive K. *Life of "Billy" Dixon, Plainsman, Scout, and Pioneer.* Dallas: P. L. Turner Co., 1914.

Dorsey, George A. *The Cheyennes.* 2 vols. Anthropological Series. Chicago: Field Columbian Museum, 1905.

Grinnell, George Bird. *The Fighting Cheyennes.* Norman: University of Oklahoma Press, 1956.

Haley, James L. *The Buffalo War: The History of the Red River Indian Uprising of 1874.* New York: Doubleday, 1976.

Hoebel, E. Adamson. *The Cheyennes: Indians of the Great Plains.* New York: Holt, Rinehart and Winston, 1960.

Hoig, Stan. *The Battle of the Washita.* Lincoln: University of Nebraska Press, 1976.

————. *The Sand Creek Massacre.* Norman: University of Oklahoma Press, 1964.

Hogarth, Andrew, and Kim Vaughn. *Battlefields, Monuments and Markers: A Guide to Native American & United States Army Engagements from 1854–1890.* Sydney: Andrew Hogarth Publishing, 1993.

————. *Cheyenne Hole.* Oberlin, Kans.: Last Indian Raid Museum, 1991.

Hutton, Paul A. *Phil Sheridan and His Army.* Lincoln: University of Nebraska Press, 1985.

Hyde, George E. *Life of George Bent Written from His Letters.* Edited by Savoie Lottinville. Norman: University of Oklahoma Press, 1968.

Jones, Douglas C. *The Treaty of Medicine Lodge.* Norman: University of Oklahoma Press, 1966.

King, James T. *War Eagle: A Life of General Eugene A. Carr.* Lincoln: University of Nebraska Press, 1963.

Leckie, William H. *The Military Conquest of the Southern Plains.* Norman: University of Oklahoma Press, 1963.

Lockard, F. M. *The History of the Early Settlement of Norton County, Kansas.* Norton, Kans.: Champion Press, 1894.

McCoy, Sondra Van Meter, and Jan Hults. *1001 Kansas Place Names.* Lawrence: University Press of Kansas, 1989.

McHugh, Tom. *The Time of the Buffalo.* Lincoln: University of Nebraska Press, 1979.

Mead, James R. *Hunting and Trading on the Great Plains, 1859–1875.* Norman: University of Oklahoma Press, 1986.

Mendoza, Patrick M. *Song of Sorrow: Massacre at Sand Creek.* Denver: Willow Wind Publishing Co., 1993.

Meredith, Grace E. *Girl Captives of the Cheyennes: A True Story of the Capture and Rescue of Four Frontier Girls.* Los Angeles: Gem Publishing Co., 1927.

Miles, General Nelson A. *Personal Recollections & Observations of General Nelson A. Miles.* 2 vols. Lincoln: University of Nebraska Press, 1992.

Miner, Craig. *West of Wichita: Settling the High Plains of Kansas, 1865–1890.* Lawrence: University Press of Kansas, 1986.

Monnett, John H. *The Battle of Beecher Island and the Indian War of 1867–1869.* Niwot: University Press of Colorado, 1992.

Nye, W. S. *Carbine & Lance: The Story of Old Fort Sill.* Norman: University of Oklahoma Press, 1937.

Powell, Peter John. *People of the Sacred Mountain: A History of the Northern Cheyenne Chiefs and Warrior Societies, 1830–1879, With an Epilogue, 1969–1974.* 2 vols. San Francisco: Harper & Row, 1981.

————. *Sweet Medicine: The Continuing Role of the Sacred Arrows, the Sun Dance, and the Sacred Buffalo Hat in Northern Cheyenne History.* 2 vols. Norman: University of Oklahoma Press, 1969.

Rankin, Charles E., ed. *Legacy: New Perspectives on the Battle of the Little Bighorn*. Helena: Montana Historical Society Press, 1996.

Sandoz, Mari. *Cheyenne Autumn*. New York: Avon Books, 1964.

Socolofsky, Homer E., and Huber Self. *Historical Atlas of Kansas*. 2nd. ed. Norman: University of Oklahoma Press, 1988.

Stands in Timber, John, and Margot Liberty. *Cheyenne Memories*. New Haven: Yale University Press, 1967.

Szabo, Joyce M. *Howling Wolf and the History of Ledger Art*. Albuquerque: University of New Mexico Press, 1994.

Utley, Robert M. *Frontier Regulars: The United States Army and the Indian, 1866–1891*. Lincoln: University of Nebraska Press, 1984.

———. *The Indian Frontier of the American West, 1846–1890*. Albuquerque: University of New Mexico Press, 1984.

Way, Thomas E., ed. *Sgt. Fred Platten's Ten Years on the Trail of the Redskins*. Williams, Ariz.: Williams News Press, 1959.

Wheeler, Homer W. *Buffalo Days*. Indianapolis: Bobbs-Merrill, 1925.

———. *The Frontier Trail: A Personal Narrative by Col. Homer W. Wheeler, Famous Frontiersman*. Los Angeles: Times-Mirror Press, 1923.

White, Richard. *It's Your Misfortune and None of My Own: A New History of the American West*. Norman: University of Oklahoma Press, 1991.

Zornow, William F. *Kansas: A History of the Jayhawk State*. Norman: University of Oklahoma Press, 1957.

Index